HEPTA
GRAM

HEPTA GRAM

The 7-Pillar Design System for the 21ˢᵗ Century

PAMELA AYUSO

HEPTAGRAM

For José, my husband and the best partner.

And for Abigail, Amanda, and Alicia,
who taught me what endless love is.

v

Table of Contents

Introduction to
The Heptagram Method

> Things of this World are in so constant a Flux, that nothing remains long in the same State. Thus People, Riches, Trade, Power, change their Stations; flourishing mighty Cities come to ruine, and prove in time neglected desolate Corners, whilst other unfrequented places grow into populous Countries, fill'd with Wealth and Inhabitants.
>
> – John Locke

Starting a business today involves facing greater challenges than ever before. Building strong organizations that can grow, adapt, and improve as the world evolves is no easy task. But with the right tools, we can create resilient organizations that can function effectively in their context and exist as learning machines.

I have been a real estate developer in Honduras for more than 13 years, with executive leadership experience in two of the most successful developers in that country – Alianza and Celaque.

At Alianza, I was responsible for managing more than $50 million in commercial and residential real estate properties. I implemented the company's operational structure, oversaw its operations and processes, and collaborated in the design and development of new commercial and residential projects throughout the capital of Tegucigalpa.

Next, my partner and I started Celaque, where we manage a portfolio of more than 200,000 square feet. We are currently building commercial and residential projects totaling over 315,000 square feet in addition to developing other projects that are around double that in size. My goal has been to grow Celaque into a model for the 21st Century.

As I restructured Alianza and built Celaque from the ground up, I developed Heptagram, a business design system based on seven pillars:

Structure, Processes, IT, Metrics, Trust, Self-Learning, and Plasticity. I wrote this book to share this step-by-step method for building robust and sustainable companies for the 21st century.

Everything contained in these pages has been tested in the real world. It is not a simple how-to guide; it is a comprehensive system to build efficient, scalable, and adaptable organizations. I have tried to lay the foundations of a living organism that is emergence-ready, a type of company that will learn from its environment and its internal behaviors.

A business that has become strong through the seven points of Heptagram will be able to respond to as-yet-unknown challenges. It has been this robust design that has enabled Celaque to thrive despite the most unexpected of all crises, the COVID-19 pandemic.

Heptagram is not a method to create a certain type of company with a fixed set of properties. It is focused on the properties of an organization's relationships with its environment and the internal relationships that determine its identity.

Developing the Heptagram method was a lengthy process. My Columbia master's degree gave me a solid background, but learning how to build a sustainable company was a challenging endeavor.

During my first years at Alianza, I managed its sales and operations. I started out by developing an efficient sales process and ultimately setting up its entire operational infrastructure. When we closed Alianza, I took much of what I had learned during that process and built my dream company, Celaque, in 2015.

Celaque develops and constructs residential and office buildings in Tegucigalpa, my hometown. It began as a property manager, but we knew it would become a real estate development company within two years. Our first hire, whom I will call Stephanie, was fresh out of college with a business administration degree. In the early days of Celaque, she and I managed all the company's operations. Through what I would later call Heptagram, I was able to turn a modest building management business with a few employees into a property development powerhouse that drives real estate trends across Central America.

We grew our organization from that initial phase to include engineers, architects, property managers, financial analysts, accountants, human resources experts, and marketers. We increased our capabilities, and Celaque now manages a broad property portfolio and builds and develops several residential and commercial projects.

Between the two companies, Alianza and Celaque, I am proud to say we have changed Tegucigalpa's skyline.

We have helped our local economy grow by providing better infrastructure with previously missing features, such as ample parking and well-designed interiors. Entrepreneurs have developed new businesses simply because our buildings exist. For example, one of our most successful complexes, Metropolis, became a magnet for orthodontists and dentists. Supporting companies also sprung up to serve this community in areas such as specialized x-rays and the sale of instruments and materials.

My work has not only centered around ensuring the company is growing and putting out the best products we can for our customers. I have also focused on building a company that is scalable, effective, self-sustaining, and human.

Celaque continues to be a work in progress, and every day we strive to make it better. Over the years, I have used the company I run as a laboratory to test ideas from both academic concepts and recent theories and trends. Through trial and error, I have tried to make sense of the world and business context we inhabit.

The solutions I have found have been the result of research and experimenting. Some things have worked, and others have failed. Although failure is always a disappointment, it has taught me many lessons about creating a results-oriented and resilient organization. Our education did not prepare us for the world we inhabit, and I discovered early on that constant learning is critical to thriving in an evolving landscape.

The first of the seven pillars of the business design Heptagram is a robust organizational structure. How you build that structure depends on your circumstances and what works best in your industry.

You can build an organizational structure or alter the company's existing configuration to be the right fit for how you function internally and externally. Your company's structure is the skeleton upon which you build everything else. Decentralizing is critical to being able to respond quickly. Along with autonomy comes trust: trust that your company has the right team and that everyone will react in the best way possible.

While responding to the various inside and outside forces, ensuring that the regular company operations are running as expected is vital. Processes are Heptagram's second pillar. Efficient processes will help you stay on track to reaching the results the company seeks. They are layered on top of your organization's structure and will ensure its effectiveness.

When I first started working at Alianza, we were a small company with a core group of fewer than ten people. As we grew, I realized the importance of processes. Actions that seem as simple as making sure all payments go out monthly need to be supported by procedures.

The third pillar consists of information systems used to program your company's processes and ensure they flow smoothly. They manage the company's workflows, store the necessary information, and operate the organization's transactions.

The fourth ingredient is metrics, a tool that goes hand in hand with the information systems and processes you implement. Metrics will keep track of important milestones and levers that indicate how the company is doing and help you stay on track to make sure you are accomplishing the main company objectives.

At Celaque, we have spent a great deal of time setting up our information systems infrastructure to properly support our processes and produce the metrics we need to run the company. We have gone through many iterations as we have improved upon the company's platform. We have added new systems, eliminated others, and modified the balance. The quality of our operations and my peace of mind have increased as we support more of our activities through technology and excellent procedures.

Trust is next. This is a complex concept, and so is the chapter I have devoted to Heptagram's fifth pillar. Without trust within the organization and between the organization and its environment, your processes and systems will not realize their maximum potential. Over the years, I have developed methods to foster trust within our organization.

The sixth and seventh pillars, self-learning and plasticity, are deeply interconnected. Being able to make sense of the context that surrounds your company is a critical competence. The settings we must respond to, and live within, are often complex scenarios, where events are interrelated and do not respond to linear assessments. Becoming adept at learning, adapting, and evolving with the changes coming our way is necessary and can be a source of growth. Your company can also be a sponge that takes in your industry's best practices and learns from mistakes. Deep wells of knowledge already exist in your organization; learning how to leverage it can create virtuous cycles of growth and advantages relative to others in your industry. Being able to respond to the jungle out there is an advantage. Everyone has a sense of a constantly evolving context, including your clients, and your company can offer them a respite from the feeling of constant change.

Plasticity is only possible through self-learning, and this book also goes deep into techniques and best practices to achieve it. The world we live in continues to shift and these changes provide opportunities for new business ideas all the time. I used to think that everything was already created, and there was not much space for true innovation. Now I know that the opposite is true; there is always room for new ideas. Established companies with more rigid structures may miss the gaps that have become recently available for businesses to solve. A company that is focused on maintaining plasticity will be in a position to turn many a threat into a miraculous opportunity.

There are multiple approaches to managing a business. Like Ray Dalio's *Principles*, some recommend establishing the company's guiding principles and then managing the company based on them. Others suggest a systemic approach, where you identify the behaviors you want to see in the company and provide the environment and incentives to make those behaviors emerge.

The amount of information is vast; it is difficult to sift through what is essential and what is not relevant for our companies. Some of the advice we receive may be dated or just a fad. If you manage a small to medium-sized company, the Heptagram method can provide useful guidance because you will likely not have access to all the resources, personnel, and consulting services that a larger enterprise can count on to design and improve its systems.

In the end, it is about finding the right combination of timeless principles and fresh business ideas that will work for your organization. Every company is different, with diverse geographic locations and industries. Even for businesses in the same industry and city, each culture and focus is different. What works in one company may be a failure in the next. The key is learning and experimenting.

*Heptagram, The 7-Pillar Business Design System for the 21*st *Century* contains a set of concepts that have worked well for me in building Celaque. I have found this mix of ideas through research and trial and error. They are, in many cases, academic, but they have also been proven in daily practice. In the book, I iterate between high-level conceptual and hands-on information, which mirrors how I have worked at Celaque. Together, they make up the program we continue to follow. I hope the Heptagram model will be as helpful for you as it has been for me to make sense of this world of constant business disruption and build a sustainable, multimillion-dollar business in the midst of it all.

WORKBOOK

I created a workbook to accompany you through your Heptagram journey. Please download it at www.pamelaayuso.com/heptagram-bonus. It has practical steps for implementing the Heptagram model in your company, bonus material, and space to keep track of your key takeaways. I have also included checklists and additional content that you can download at www.pamelaayuso.com/heptagram-bonus.

My Story

From Immigrant Student to Trailblazing CEO

> It is good to have an end to journey toward, but it is the journey that matters in the end.
>
> — Ursula K. Le Guin

I am the co-founder and CEO of Celaque, one of the largest real estate building developers in Honduras. The real estate industry, here and in the rest of the world, has tended to be traditional and conservative, something I did not want for Celaque. My task has been to build a modern, successful developer in a country that is still in development.

Honduras has been chiefly an export-oriented country. It is located in the heart of Central America, a region of more than 45 million people. It is a dynamic area with a younger, increasingly globalized population. Our communications infrastructure was not quite at the same level as that of wealthier countries when the new technologies arrived, and we have quickly adopted innovations.

Riding this new wave of technology, I designed and managed the operations of Alianza—once one of the country's most prominent developers—and then built Celaque, its successor. I used both companies as laboratories to experiment with my seven-pillar method, Heptagram, based on the best practices of leading companies worldwide.

I was born in Guatemala City. My father was an entrepreneur with an MBA and a background in chemical engineering. My mother was initially a stay-at-home mom who had studied business administration.

Sadly, my father passed away when I was five years old, and we moved to Tegucigalpa, Honduras, my mother's hometown. My mom also became an entrepreneur in Honduras, starting a crafts store, which she still manages.

Growing up, my mom had us take as many extracurricular activities as possible. I took classes in pottery, painting, piano, embroidery, and French. When I was not in school or taking classes, I read. We lived with my grandparents, so, luckily, I had access to my grandfather's and my aunt's old books.

I tried to get my hands on as many books as possible, and I read voraciously every year until I finished school. Even though I lost my reading habit in my twenties as I finished college and started to work, it was always an essential part of my identity. When I became an entrepreneur, I was gradually able to get back into the routine of reading. I am again reading as much as I possibly can, sometimes as many as four books a month.

When I graduated from high school, I was accepted to Ithaca College with a partial tuition scholarship. It was an exciting time. I had never lived alone before, and I was setting off to live in a different country with almost no communication with my family back home.

I had never seen snow before and was looking forward to experiencing it for the first time. Little did I realize how different the weather would be in upstate New York from the temperate and warm climate in the city where I had grown up. The cold weather did have one advantage; I mostly worked and studied with few distractions during those long winter months.

At the end of my junior year, it was time to start thinking about life after school. I knew I wanted to get some experience in the United States, so I searched for an internship, knowing that that was the surest path to a permanent position after graduation.

I can still picture the enormous spreadsheet I put together, where I kept track of all the places where I applied. It was one of the most anxious periods in my life. It was not easy for an international student to find a paid internship that would later lead to a job. My spreadsheet had multiple columns detailing the companies I was applying to, when I had sent the applications, any follow-up information, and the outcomes.

The spreadsheet quickly numbered more than 100 sent applications. I received rejection after rejection, which I dutifully entered on my spreadsheet. Finally, I had a phone interview with Ernst & Young (now EY), which went well.

I rode five hours on a bus to New York for my final interview and fell in love with the company. I was also offered an internship position with Andersen, another of the "Big Five" accounting companies (at the time). I accepted Ernst & Young's offer to join their internship program as a financial auditor.

After a great internship, I returned to my final year at school. By that point, I had a full scholarship and was saving money. I graduated Summa Cum Laude in 2002 with a double major in Accounting and Finance. Fortunately, my worries about my professional future were over because early in the year, I accepted Ernst & Young's offer to work full-time as an auditor in their Manhattan office in Times Square. To me, it was a dream come true to live and work in New York.

During the next three years, I learned and grew more than I would have ever imagined. Living alone in New York, I learned about work and life: from discovering how to negotiate with a landlord who would turn off my heat at night to auditing some of the biggest financial services firms during that time, like UBS and Lehman Brothers. I went from being a Staff to a Senior Auditor and became a Certified Public Accountant (CPA).

Through our audit work, I became familiar with how the companies we examined created processes and controls and mitigated risk. I also learned how these big companies worked and how they differed. I practiced being adaptable as I changed physical locations every few months, and each year, moved from team to team both in the companies we audited and in my firm.

An auditor has unusual insight into the inner workings of small and large companies, national and international. I met new people in all kinds of positions, from the CEO to the security guards at the companies I audited. Finally, during that time, I discovered what I wanted to do in the long run. I wanted to be in the front office, making the decisions and eventually running a company.

After three years as an auditor, I went to Columbia University's School of International and Public Affairs (SIPA) to study for my degree in International Finance. I did not choose a Master's in Business Administration because I wanted to balance my business degrees with a broader view of the world, which I knew that SIPA would give me. It did not disappoint me; those two years were among the most fulfilling I have ever had. I learned about economics, politics, social entrepreneurship, corporate finance, and development.

Something else happened during my years at Columbia. I started to feel a yearning to return to Honduras. I wanted to be a part of my country's growth, and I was ready. After graduating, I spent a little less than a year as the controller of a hedge fund and then decided to move back. After six years in the city, saying goodbye to New York was very hard because I had come to love it as a second home. I still do.

I first entered the world of real estate when I moved back to Honduras. My soon-to-be husband, Jose, and a partner had started a real estate development company two years earlier. Having worked in accounting and finance in New York, we discussed what I should do with my professional career in Tegucigalpa, Honduras. After searching for possibilities, my husband suggested that we work together. At the time, the company had developed only two small office buildings, but it was growing rapidly.

This moment was an inflection point for me. I could continue on my corporate path, searching out positions in accounting or finance, or I could start something new. I had always dreamed of building a company, so when Jose asked, I said yes (again). That is how I began my career in real estate.

I did not know anything about the industry and had never worked in Tegucigalpa as a professional. Everything was new to me. I tried to make myself useful at my new company and proposed building out its finance department. I quickly found out that we did not need a full team because, at that point, we were not working with financing or outside investors.

What we needed was to build our sales capabilities. My only experience in sales had been as a seasonal worker in my grandfather's toy store. Even so, sales were what we needed, so that is what I did. I became a salesperson.

At the time, we were selling Alianza's most significant office project to date, so I dived into sales and learned as I went along. I bought every single book I could find and read as much as I could. I built metrics and set goals for myself.

Every day, I called customers, and most did not call me back. I launched new marketing ideas, and they failed miserably. There were months where I had little to no sales. Suddenly, I met with a customer two or three times, and we closed a $150,000 deal.

It was a challenging time to learn how to be a real estate salesperson. In 2009, Honduras suffered a coup d'état. The country was going through its worst political crisis in decades, precisely as we were getting ready to finish the project and start selling more. As a country, our constitutional continuity had been broken. As a result, it was an uncertain time to be an investor and try to sell a building. Eventually, we had new elections, and the political climate stabilized.

Through it all, I called a friend who had also selected the time around our political crisis to build his real estate agent business. I asked him how he was doing, and he did the same. We compared our newly built metrics. "You had an amazing month!" he joked when I told him I had closed out one month at zero. I laughed. We were both learning and adapting methods we read about in books, trying to build our companies. Little did I know at the time that I would end up creating my own method, Heptagram.

Given the adverse circumstances facing our company, I realized I could not do it all myself, and I started to build a sales team. At Ernst & Young, I supervised new Staff auditors, but building a team at a new company was completely different. During this time, I started to learn about hiring and establishing an organization.

Sales and real estate became my passions. I loved negotiating and closing deals. I also loved being able to contribute to the growth of Alianza through the sales we were making. I was so devoted that I worked through my first pregnancy in 2011. The day I went into labor, I stayed at the office until 6 p.m. I then went home, and my daughter was born early the following morning on a Saturday. By the following Wednesday, I was back at the negotiating table, closing a big sale.

In the next two years, Alianza kept growing, and it was time to take the company's structure to a new level. Until that point, we had had a basic way of operating, taking care of sales and purchases as they happened but with no processes and no overall structure. It was starting to cause problems as we grew. As a CPA, I knew the first step was to invest in our accounting. At the time, Alianza had a bookkeeper, but we needed a full-fledged accounting team and supporting software.

I started by implementing no-frills accounting software and adapting it to our needs. When our accounting software was working, and I saw that I could implement software without spending on consultants, I moved on to our Customer Resource Management (CRM) system.

Although it took longer to program, our CRM took our sales process to another level. We now had on-demand, customizable reports, and we could easily search all our customers. I could also program workflows that we could follow during our sales cycle, starting with a lead and ending with a sale.

I measured my cycles in Alianza by my pregnancies. By the time I finished implementing the CRM, and I had started to launch a project management software for our firm, my second daughter was about to be born. My goal was to be done with both implementations by then.

Our project management system was how we managed the work we had to do, and it then became the system we used to organize and operate our company processes. We began to assemble procedures for accounting, office administration, and sales, a journey that took five years of iterations as we grew and improved our methodology. The final piece was bringing down barriers to sharing our documents, which we solved by implementing a company-wide, cloud-based server.

By then, we had revamped all the company operations and continued to develop new buildings that, little by little, changed Tegucigalpa. We improved our facilities with each new iteration, and I worked over the next two years on refining the systems and processes we had implemented. Whenever I found a problem in how we operated, I tried to solve it to prevent it from occurring again by including what we had learned in a process or workflow or restructuring how different parts of the company interacted.

Throughout this process, certain aspects emerged as the beating heart of a successful business. I thought a lot about integrating the company's structure, processes, IT, metrics, a culture of trust, and the concepts of plasticity and self-learning into a dynamic, synergetic whole.

Often, I encountered problems I had no idea how to solve. I did not know where to start. No education can prepare us for everything we have to face. I had to learn how to research and solve everyday problems. For example, because my background was in finance and accounting, I had no formal training in real estate sales and development. To better prepare myself, I read every book I could find. I even bought college textbooks, which I read in their entirety. I then took courses in real estate development. And if I came across a problem I could not solve, I would research it.

As the architecture of our business became more and more robust, I realized the system I was creating would not only apply to real estate. My education had exposed me to the intricacies of many industries, and I knew what I was building could also be applicable elsewhere.

While I understood early on that I was creating something new, I was also aware that this idea was the result of my own experience combined with the work of people that had gone before me. I found out that someone has already come across every question I ever had. It was only a matter of finding the right resources. I followed this mantra whenever I encountered obstacles and did not know which step to take next. For instance, when I implemented our systems, I dove into user forums and help resources.

In 2015, right before my third daughter's birth, my husband and I co-founded Celaque, and I became the CEO. For the next two years, I continued my dual roles as Director at Alianza and CEO at Celaque as we completed our final project in Alianza, a 300,000 square foot complex with office, apartment, and retail commercial space. This new venture was my golden opportunity to put Heptagram to the test. Would I succeed in creating a thriving and robust company based on the seven pillars that had led to Alianza's success? Only time would tell.

It was refreshing to start a new company. At Celaque, I was able to begin at zero. It was indeed a gift to have a chance to do that in my career. Alianza taught me about real estate and about managing and building a company, which gave me a base to develop what I knew I wanted and what I did not want. I wanted Celaque to be a 21st-century company.

One of the first things I did was experiment to find the structure that would work best for us. To avoid duplicated responsibilities, lack of accountability, and general confusion, we set up Celaque as a functional organization. We began small, and I looked for the best team we could hire.

Layered on top of that structure, which is Heptagram's first pillar, I added our processes and information systems, pillars two and three. Due to budgetary issues, we did not have an Enterprise Resource Management (ERP) system at Alianza. At Celaque, I implemented one as soon as I could. We were able to program the workflows based on the best practices we had learned at Alianza. I had also determined, based on experience, that I wanted to devote resources to areas that could be improved, so we made functions such as inventory management a priority.

Then, we worked on our product development cycle. We organized a Developments committee, which makes the decisions on new investments and our products. We improved not only the types of products we brought to market but also our procurement. We made sure we only worked with suppliers that had been responsive in past projects and created a process for negotiations. The result of our focus on the right suppliers quickly showed, because during the construction phase of our projects, we have fewer problems, and they run more smoothly.

We continue to use the tools we have implemented to build other parts of the company, such as our property management arm, which has been growing continuously. We began to use new software to manage our buildings and properties better. We have programmed enhancements to our ERP to make our billing more automatic, considering our company's peculiarities and geographic location. All these processes and cycles were punctuated by adequate metrics, pillar four of the successful business Heptagram.

Ultimately, my goal is to create a dynamic company where each team has all the tools and resources to grow. That is where the fifth pillar, trust, comes into play. Our commitment to fostering trust includes taking down the barriers to information so that everyone has all the information they need to do their work as effectively as possible. Furthermore, we have become a self-learning company, as Heptagram's sixth pillar prescribes. We try to acquire as much knowledge as we can from the world, our daily interactions, and any available opportunities for improvement, as well as the mistakes we have made.

The process has not been linear. My utopian ideas collided with reality on several occasions, but overall, I am proud of the company we have built. We have navigated a changing business context as we continue to improve our products and achieve our goals. We have achieved extraordinary plasticity, in line with Heptagram's seventh pillar. Celaque continues to evolve, and I learn every single day. I experiment as much as I can to learn more about the organization and to improve it. And we get better every year.

The COVID-19 pandemic came to test everything we had built at Celaque. This situation was the true, real-life test for the Heptagram method. The crisis found us two weeks away from the opening of a 190,000 square foot office building and in the middle of the structure of the first building in a complex of 216 apartments. We were up to the 4th floor of the 9-level building when we locked the gates to both projects and left. Simultaneously, our corporate office, comprising a team of around 30, moved to remote work that same day, with no prior preparation.

As I developed Celaque, I had no idea I was also preparing for this, our most challenging test. Because our tools have been on the cloud from our inception, all we had to do was switch to our home locations.

Like every other company that made the transition, we also had to adapt. We had never worked remotely, so we had to adjust to include new practices such as morning and afternoon meetings to review progress. Some of our teams also had to absorb members from other departments whose primary work is presence-based such as salespeople and the engineers who supervise our projects. Overall, I am happy to say that, except for our constructions, we have not stopped working and that every investment we made on flexibility and adaptability has paid off.

Leading this company has been and continues to be my greatest teacher. I have learned how to build a company and then how to trust others to see it through as we grow. I have also had to discover how to cope with growth personally and as a company to continue to expand sustainably. More recently, it taught me how to manage an unprecedented crisis. The ride has been immensely fulfilling, and I hope it will help you build and improve your company.

It is hard to tell now what came first, the Heptagram method or Celaque's unprecedented success. It has been a synergetic relationship. Starting a business that can withstand a planetary crisis is a seemingly insurmountable task. In a way, I feel it is my duty to share what I have learned. Many business books offer magical solutions. This book is not one of them. Implementing the Heptagram model takes time and hard work, but in my experience, it can help you create the company you have envisioned.

Heptagram's Seven Pillars

ONE

Structure

> All large-scale human cooperation is ultimately based on our belief in imagined orders.
>
> – Yuval Noah Harari

Designing a company is not an easy task. If you are an entrepreneur whose focus is on your product or service, you are likely not an expert on how to build a company. You also might not have the resources to hire a consulting team to advise you on putting together your company's structure and systems.

As your organization grows, you will be focused primarily on getting the work done, which may be sufficient for some time. But that may not lead your company to work to its fullest potential. I know because that is what happened to me—and unfortunately, I did not have any warning signs to tell me that the problem was in my company's design.

When we first founded Celaque, I did not know much about organizational structures. I knew we needed a set configuration and that it had to be clear to everybody within the company and outside of it. But I knew little about business design models.

As the company grew, I took on more and more responsibilities. I quickly became overextended with the amount of work that had to go through me and the level of accountability I was handling. I had not yet been able to create a clear structure where others could take care of operations while I focused on strategy and achieving the company's overall goals. I thought this occurred because I was not delegating appropriately or had not yet hired enough people. The problem, however, was that we were operating from a simple organizational structure when a functional organization would have been more appropriate.

Structure is an essential component to implement the Heptagram model successfully. It is the foundation of it all. Achieving the right balance between efficiency and flexibility will allow your company to be both resilient and scalable. A modern company's structure must be solid yet adaptable.

DESIGNING YOUR COMPANY

Organizing a company starts with determining a strategy for its direction based on a balance between the company's internal dynamics and the external forces it faces. This strategy can often be the competitive advantage a company has through its products, technology, and other resources that others cannot imitate. Strategy defines where the company will direct its limited resources, given the vast array of opportunities available.

A strategy is made up of three parts. The first involves defining a company's goals, which could be growth, increased market share, or a positive return on investment. Second, the company decides which country or location it is serving, what part of the market it wants to address, and what products it will offer. This focus can be modified as a company evolves, and it may decide to start offering its products in a different region, or it may choose to add more products. The company will have to grow and shift to accommodate these new goals.

Finally, a company will determine how it wants to measure its success. To do this, it will decide where its competitive advantage lies and the formula it will use to achieve its objectives. The business may choose a strategy that centers around its customers or its products. Pharmaceutical corporations often pursue strategies focused on patenting products to sell for many years. Companies may quickly see their competitive advantages lapse in our fast-moving world, and the organization will need to shift.

At Celaque, we currently serve only one city, Tegucigalpa. We are often asked to move our operation into other cities, especially Honduras's other big city, San Pedro Sula. Though tempting, we believe we have more than enough space left to grow in our current location before moving to the next. Nevertheless, if and when we do expand geographically, our company structure would have to become different. Our team would grow, and each person's responsibilities would shift as some of our managers would have to supervise more than one region.

We have evolved our strategy, however, by expanding into different segments of the market. When we moved into the residential market, after serving only the office market initially, we had to learn how to manage these types of buildings, for example.

The challenges inherent in managing buildings that house more than 100 families are different from those we face in the caretaking of office buildings. In office buildings, our peak times are during regular business hours, which is the opposite in residential buildings, where most of the activity occurs when our residents are not at work.

Furthermore, in our apartment buildings, we have common areas that become extensions of people's homes. For instance, we have public living room areas where people host their families and friends, or we manage a play area for children. People receive guests at any time of the day. An apartment building is their home, and our level of service must reflect that. To better communicate with our clients, maintain common residential areas, and manage their events and packages, we had to implement a series of processes and software we had never used in the past. We also had to hire specialized maintenance and reception staff for the buildings.

Once a strategy is set, the company can then select the best organizational structure to fulfill its goals. The organization's architecture identifies how the company's hierarchy works and how to configure it. And with this frame in place, the relevant systems and processes are defined, which is how the work gets done in a company. These can be company-wide or applicable only to a functional area.[1]

If the company has limited reserves, it must decide what it will do and what it will not do. And the fewer the resources are, the more precise the strategy must be. If the business environment shifts, so should the company's approach to taking advantage of new opportunities.[2] In the end, a strategy is how firms plan to create value, whether it is lower costs or better products.[3] The strategy guides how a company is structured, its processes, and what kind of team it needs.[4]

Our strategy at Celaque was to grow in asset size in Tegucigalpa by creating value in residential and office buildings for our customers. To achieve that, we designed a structure that could handle our expansion. First, we settled on a functional organization. Then, we invested heavily in our processes. For instance, we improved our procedures so that the type of work we were doing in one project could be replicated in others in the future. We could easily have reinvented the way we did things with each new project, but doing so would not have been efficient or a good use of our team's time.

We also wanted to create a learning culture so that our team was continually improving how we operated. We know that with each building's construction, we learn how to do things better on the next project, and that improves our workflow overall.

We continue to hone how we operate to attain our growth objective. Not only has our company infrastructure adapted to our mandate, but we have increased the number of people on our team in preparation for the growth. We have also been training our teams to make sure they are ready when we expand.

Conversely, if we did not want to grow and instead sought only to manage the properties we already handle, we would have a different structure and a smaller and different team. We would need to have maybe one or two engineers on staff to handle remodels as opposed to the many that work during the construction phase of each of our new building projects.

A strategy is the starting point that determines how you will organize the company. Sometimes, you may not have explicitly stated your policy, but taking the time to define it will help you build or reconfigure the skeleton for the rest of the company. Then, the proper structure will determine the types of results your company will have.

Types of Structures

Building a company's organizational structure is one of the most important investments any business leader can make. It also requires many hours of work and design. The efforts must be continuously calibrated as the internal operations change and the outside world in which it exists shifts to different realities.

The skeleton that holds all company operations, the organizational structure is the basis of how a company is constructed. It is the essential architecture that defines how tasks are subdivided and managed within an organization.[5] A strong structure will let your company run fluidly and efficiently by clearly designating which team is responsible for what and how each of these roles fits into the grand scheme of the organization. This way, tasks are accomplished without anyone getting in anyone's way, and there is a greatly diminished probability that an important task will get lost.

All companies are hierarchies, even the most benign, and a structure takes the ambiguity out of how they are organized. Work is achieved in an organization when it is parsed out to different groups, and a configuration ensures that they come together coherently.[6]

Research has shown that a company's performance stems from how well its organization's architecture was designed to fit its needs.[7] When creating a company, its leaders need to consider internal as well as external factors. The structure should accommodate the company's management style and its level of centralization or decentralization. It ought to also respond to the external environment and the current business climate. The firm will perform its best when there is an excellent internal to external fit, and it can respond to outside factors.[8]

A company's organization can depend on its industry, size, culture, geographic reach, and stage of development. Its design should consider the company's goals, strategy, and structure and the human dimension, its processes and teams, and how they work together.[9]

The four main structures you can use for your company are:

- **Simple**: tasks are assigned as needed, and the company's leader coordinates all the work
- **Functional**: the company is organized by specialized functions
- **Divisional**: the configuration is determined by a product/service, market/customer, or geographic location that the firm serves
- **Matrix**: a combination of functional and divisional focus.

Each of these arrangements favors an emphasis on product, service, and/or customer service orientation and functional specialization. A company focused on the customer or a product, with departments named accordingly, has a strong external focus and would be organized as a Divisional or Matrix organization.

A company with departments named after a function will organize its work around specific activities, and its focus will be more internal. A more functional company will have marketing and finance departments, for instance. Defining an organizational structure is essential because how we organize the company determines how we will subdivide the work and then how we will manage operations.

This chart defines each of the types of organizations by preference.

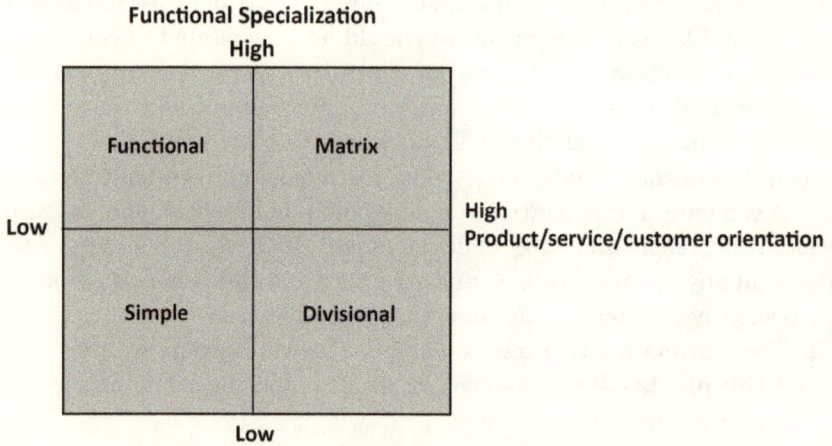

Functional Specialization
High

Functional	Matrix
Simple	Divisional

Low

High
Product/service/customer orientation

Low

Figure 1. Types of organizations by preference.[10]

Depending on the needs of the company, we can combine these different configurations within an organization. For example, a company can have one Functional part, another that is Simple, and another organized as a Matrix.[11]

Simple

The four structures come into play after a company has advanced to a certain level. Before that, almost all businesses, once they begin, naturally fall into a Simple structure in which the company's leader assigns all the tasks as they are needed, and there are no permanent assignments or work descriptions. The work is fluid and constrained to however much the leader can process. The job is demanding because she must supervise everything and be at the center of everything. This type of organizational structure is typical of small companies in a start-up phase, but it can also be seen in established companies without growth strategy.

My mother-in-law's company manages two apartment buildings and several houses. Her organization has a Simple structure, and her team includes an administrator and a building superintendent. All decisions go through her in this small operation that has been in business for many years. This Simple organization works perfectly and fulfills its goals and strategy.

Functional

As a company starts to have more success and expands its output and the number of workers it employs, the need will arise for a more complex structure that will help it operate more efficiently to handle this increased demand. If the company sells one main product that now needs the support of different departments, such as manufacturing, marketing, and sales, the next step is to create a Functional organization, which is ideal for supporting the people heading up these various areas.

These different departments are led by a manager who coordinates the subgroups' assigned responsibilities. The work flows from one unit to the next, and each group must coordinate with the others to keep the flow moving.[12] When organizations are new, and once they have outgrown a Simple structure, they usually begin with a Functional structure centered around one business strategy.[13]

In Functional organizations, less is demanded of the company's leader, even though he still coordinates and plans its actions. Functional organizations increase the company's efficiency because the teams become specialized by type of activity, and that aids them in organizing their tasks together.

The Functional structure, which began with specialization dating back to Adam Smith, is the most common organization, and it mirrors how our world is organized. University departments are divided by functions. For example, they train accountants and marketing professionals, so it makes sense for companies to follow those same divisions.

The number of departments varies by company. At Google, to decrease the likelihood of micromanaging, managers had a minimum of seven reports.[14] Richard Burton et al. recommend having between five and seven units. The more there are, the more onerous the demand on the company's executive is. Not only is the person more likely to become overtaxed, but as the number of departments increases, the needs for coordination also grow nonlinearly.[15] Furthermore, teams within the company and outsiders may have more trouble distinguishing who is responsible for what. At Celaque, my goal was to keep the structure as simple as possible without oversimplifying it, so we ended up with five departments.

In my experience, the best number of departments also depends on the stage of a company's evolution. At the beginning of our growth, when I was managing six separate departments and working with our team to set up the company, I found that more than six would have been too complicated for me to handle. Now that we have developed each department and have management tools, such as metrics and budgets for each, I am considering splitting one department into two. In a more stable company, it is easier to manage more areas.

Functional organizations are specialized. Traditionally, they used to have more management levels; in the past, a middle management layer was added to perform operations. Information technology has enabled a more horizontal approach by removing this middle layer.

A Functional organization is useful for a business that involves high volumes of tasks that are regularly repeated.[16] The repetition reinforces the teams' knowledge of each other, and it sharpens their ability to collaborate.

In *How Google Works*, Eric Schmidt and Jonathan Rosenberg recommend maintaining a Functional structure made up of departments such as engineering, products, and finance that report directly to the CEO for as long as possible. This type of organization results in a free flow of information and people.[17]

Divisional

A Divisional organization is, in some ways, the opposite of a Functional structure. Divisional focuses on a product or service or a customer or market.[18] Picture an energy services company that starts by producing energy through hydroelectric plants. It begins with a Functional structure divided into departments such as accounting, sales, and legal to support the construction of the plants and the sale of the energy produced.

The company is very successful in building plants but cannot grow with that product because there is a limit to hydroelectric power demand. They see a need for gas stations in their region and decide to diversify to include this new product offering. The two products are different, so the company chooses to reorganize divisionally. Now, there are two separate units organized to support two different types of products. Each division can choose to structure itself to respond in the best way to the markets it serves.

In a different scenario, the company could have decided to grow instead, not through its product offering but geographically. Perhaps when it realized it had no more room to build more hydroelectric plants in its region, it decided it was time to move to another country. In that case, the company may have chosen to reorganize itself into a Divisional structure based on geographic areas. Each division, again, would be set up to best support the sales of hydroelectric energy in each of the locations it serves.

Usually, when a company follows its original business strategy but growth stalls, it seeks to grow by adding new products and services or going into other markets. When the company grows in this direction, it makes sense to evolve to a Divisional organization[19] to better respond to the new demands.

In a Divisional configuration, each sub-unit is independent (though they follow the policies dictated by headquarters). The divisions can be called strategic business units, profit centers, or product, customer, or country businesses. Each group has a financial goal.

The company's top executive may be very involved, directing everything the division does, or the leader's participation may be limited to financial supervision. This type of organization works best in the latter case, as too much involvement may decrease efficiency.

Divisions are autonomous; in other words, each division's leader can operate independently, taking the actions she deems most effective to best respond to a customer's demands or market. The division's manager organizes it in response to its market—most are internally structured as a Simple or Functional organization—whatever works best to move as quickly and effectively as possible. Therefore, a company with a Divisional structure is more adaptable. It can change internally (e.g., types and number of internal departments or roles within the organization) in the context of a changing business environment where new competitors might have come in, or the market is demanding different types of products.

The disadvantage is that internal company collaboration suffers because each subdivision is independent of the other. Therefore, a company can have two Human Resources (HR) departments that use different methodologies to manage each of the division's talent and do not collaborate. These dynamics can create silos, where valuable information stays within a team or department and is not shared company-wide. Silos can prove inefficient in the long run because they may cause processes and ideas to become duplicated, and departments do not learn from their counterparts' experiences.

Furthermore, the customer may need to take on the brunt of coordinating between two different divisions in the same company. When the company manages the divisions separately, the disadvantage is that they may not work together. Customers need to speak to each of them independently as if they were dealing with two different organizations.

A company can continue to grow using a Divisional configuration by adding as many divisions as is necessary.

Matrix

Another type of configuration is the Matrix structure, which also works well for companies with a product/market orientation. The additional advantage is that a Matrix organization also has a high functional specialization orientation. The company combines a Divisional structure on one side of its organization with a Functional structure on the other. The company's chief executive must oversee both configurations, making sure to resolve conflicts between them.

A Matrix organization can be flexible and can quickly adapt to new situations. It is efficient because it is Functional and effective because it is Divisional. If it is not well-managed, conflicts between horizontal and vertical units, too much information and meetings, and slow decision-making can lead to paralysis. Executives must focus on the whole picture of the company while also watching each division or function. Matrix organizations are a good option when companies operate in an external business environment that constantly changes and is hard to predict.[20]

Unlike in a traditional functional hierarchy, in a Matrix organization, power is shared between two kinds of managers. One manager defines the work that needs to be accomplished to deliver on a product, project, or customer, often called a project manager. The other, the functional manager, distributes resources related to his technical department (e.g., marketing or finance). He defines how and where the task will be done and by whom, for example. Whereas a project manager will determine what work needs to be done, by when, and why.[21]

In this type of structure, functional and project managers must know clearly who does what and when because otherwise, the structure's complexity may cause more problems than it solves. To avoid nonconstructive conflict, managers need to have a broader institutional perspective, realizing that everyone contributes to the strength of the entire company.[22] The structure's architecture ensures that everyone knows to whom they are reporting.

A Matrix organization works best if it only has two sides so that each person will have only two managers to work with—such as a project manager and a function manager. More than that will make an already complicated structure harder to manage. Nested matrices, one matrix inside of another, are best avoided because they can add unwanted complexity. The Harvard Business Review has described matrix structures as "a prophylactic against corporate silos."[23]

Heptagram advocates simplicity whenever possible. Matrix structures should be reserved for companies where coordination between unit and team managers is required daily. In other cases, a hard-wired matrix is not needed, and soft-wiring (i.e., spontaneous coordination between middle managers) can do the trick.

A Company's Evolution

You may choose to organize your company by function or by division. Whatever model works best for your business, it is important to design its structure intentionally. However, for a growing company, the complexity is immense as workloads increase.

Often, a company will be in a growth stage and encountering problems—for example, a vital activity will not be completed on time, such as a client proposal going out too late or, if a company's marketing strategy is based on social media, its content calendar may not be consistent enough. The company's leaders may not realize that the problem is an organizational structure that is not properly supporting the teams to operate and respond to the company's demands.

Finding the configuration that works for your company is not a one-time event. You may have selected the perfect structure when you started, but as your company expanded to include additional employees, it will outgrow that initial framework. That's why companies must be continuously analyzed and restructured to satisfy the inevitable changes that come within every business. The entire structure may not need to be adjusted, but it might be necessary to create a new unit or combine two departments. If the work is not flowing smoothly or there are frequent delays, it is always a good idea to look at the company's configuration as the possible source of the problem.

We organized Celaque by function—but it did not start that way. We founded the company with a Simple structure with me, the executive, managing the work of initially, one employee, and then a few more people. I knew everything that was happening and approved all decisions.

We were mainly a property manager, and our structure worked well initially. I implemented many changes and innovations—our small size made us very agile. Then we started designing and building our first development project, Astria, a 138-unit apartment building.

The type and quantity of work we now needed to accomplish became more complicated, and we had to evolve. We needed to have a team made up of architects and engineers to build the project, and the addition of that department meant we had to move to a more Functional structure. As construction on the building began, we had to consolidate our finance and accounting teams into one department to manage the project loans and other transactions.

Still, as we grew into a Functional organization, I managed and supervised all the work. Little by little, I assigned tasks and identified responsibilities but nevertheless remained the primary supervisor. Most approvals went through me, and I tried to know everything that was happening. We were an amalgamation of a Simple and a Functional structure.

It was not long before this combination stopped working. I was becoming a bottleneck, and we needed to become a Functional organization. I did not realize this until later, but I was working with a structure that no longer addressed our needs. Luckily, we continued to take actions that eventually took us into becoming the organization we wanted to be.

Gradually, we transitioned fully into a Functional organization, where all the company's functions were carefully mapped, placed within the suitable unit, and streamlined. We were a small company with a single product, so we decided a Functional organization would be the best option for us at this stage. We strove to ensure that the units encompassed all the possible activities within a company but did not overlap. Each group's function became specialized.

We organized the company into five departments. Two are specific to the real estate industry—Developments and Properties—and the others are common to any industry:

- Corporate: this department handles strategy, reporting, company-wide policies, systems and processes, and HR.
- Finance: accounting, legal, and relationships with banks and investors.
- Developments: design, launch, and construction of our buildings.
- Properties: management of our existing office, residential and retail commercial spaces, as well as the buildings we have developed.
- Sales: sales and leasing of our new projects and our property portfolio.

Although the general functional categories are available in any textbook, finding the ones that would adapt in the best way to our company and industry required considerable analysis. Furthermore, we simultaneously implemented an Enterprise Resource Planning (ERP) solution, which required that we organize each of our different transactions by department, adding more pressure to define what went where. After researching how other real estate developers organize themselves, I discovered a structure that I thought would work well for us and used it as a model for the five departments we currently have.

Refining Structures

We have found that most of the work we do fits neatly within these five categories, and we have been placing each of the company's functions within them. Whenever we come across a task that does not fall within one of the departments, we ask where it makes the most sense for it to reside.

The goal is that each activity is streamlined and that it's clear from the beginning who is responsible for each task. Once it is placed within a department, we also ask how a given activity might affect the following department and how it fits within the broader company. True to the promise of a Functional organization, by placing each task into one of our departments, we have made the work we perform more efficient.

Sometimes, we find that we had initially managed a role in one department, yet it no longer makes any sense there, so we move it. If we find something that does not flow smoothly, we adjust it immediately. At other times, we organize the role or responsibility around a person's strengths.

After we established our Functional organization, the flow of our work improved significantly. Each department is clear about its responsibilities and how tasks connect between one area and the next.

It is not easy to move a company from one organizational structure to another. However, if your current organization does not fit your company's strategy and is causing you problems, it is worth the effort to reconfigure it. You will not regret it.

ORGANIZATIONAL STRUCTURE TIPS

Having started my company with a Simple structure and then moving on to a Functional organization, I learned as I experimented. Throughout that transition, I found some overarching concepts that I applied to Celaque. These ideas helped me craft the structure that has worked well for us and is flexible enough to help us continue growing.

For Functional Configurations

If you choose a Functional configuration as we did, responsibilities are best grouped by type. A company can adopt a structure that ensures that each person within a team is responsible for processes from beginning to end. We have experimented with designing roles so that people can perform most of the functions assigned to a department. The opposite would be specializing and focusing on a very narrow set of individual tasks.

How a company manages client relationships is a simple example. To integrate the full process, one person would be responsible for maintaining the entire relationship with a customer from invoicing to customer service requests rather than only producing invoices. That way, ensuring the delivery of invoices, providing customer service related to them, and receiving payments will be part of one team's responsibility.

Otherwise, when we assign tasks across different teams or departments, it is less efficient, duplication occurs, and some things are left undone. For example, with customer service, a client is better served when she has one point of reference for her needs and avoids the frustration of going to different people for help with an invoice and a product or service complaint.

Even though duplicating functions across various roles at Celaque might increase accuracy by providing more than one person's input, we avoid doing that because it results in inefficient overall design. Some processes cross departments, of course. If an operation can fit within a department, we prefer to keep it there.

Also, when the work operates in only one place, responsibility is always more evident. Within each department, the duties should be clearly defined and grouped in ways that make sense for your company. Each team member will know which department handles each transaction and whom to speak to with a question or issue to resolve. Problems, therefore, are addressed more efficiently, and less time is lost searching for a person who can help.

This same concept applies to more complex responsibilities, such as producing reports and leading improvements in each area of the business, where each team is responsible for managing the depth of these tasks. The idea is for the information needed to modify and improve the final product to be as close and available to the user as possible.

The Right Departments

It is crucial to determine what departments your company needs to meet your strategy, goals, industry, culture, and history. When I first ran operations for Alianza, we had four departments: Sales, Sales Administration and Marketing, Projects, and Administration. We had an outside accountant—who reported to Administration—even when our transaction volume justified hiring an in-house accountant.

Quickly, we discovered that some essential functions like purchasing and the design of our projects did not fit within any of these four departments. Eventually, we hired an engineer to manage purchasing and design, and we added these as separate departments.

We also did not have a formal reporting structure to an executive and instead functioned as a partnership. This situation occurred because initially, we envisioned the company as a vehicle for managing each project as it arose. This lack of organization caused us to spend much time solving problems that we could have prevented and recreating the necessary resources to resolve them as they arose. Without specific managers responsible for each department, the partners took turns as problem-solvers.

Having the right departments is vital. It takes time to refine, and sometimes, you may spend some time with a set of departments before you realize that your structure needs to change significantly. When we founded Celaque, we improved the departments we had at Alianza. We split the Administration department into two: Finance and Corporate. We then combined Sales Administration with Property Management to create Properties.

Flat Structures

The world is moving to flatter structures with wider spans, and companies are designing structures with fewer levels of supervision. As we leave behind command styles of leadership, managers can supervise more people, resulting in flatter structures, faster decisions, faster feedback loops to decision-makers, and lower costs.[24]

In a traditional command structure, someone is at the helm with the answers and know-how to direct the information and supervise actions. The controlled movement of data can cause mistakes because our shifting world makes it hard to foresee who will need what information at what time.

In a traditional structure, data is coming in from all directions because our world is more interconnected than ever. As technology continues to break down barriers to information, knowledge moves faster and faster. An interrelated world creates opportunities all around, and we can achieve things today in seconds that were never possible before. As miraculous as this is, it also makes us vulnerable. One broken link in this chain of information can have unforeseen repercussions.

Centralizing all decision-making in a manager, for instance, presupposes an optimum way for information to flow and that you cannot trust everyone in the institution with this knowledge. Having a flatter structure is an attempt to tear down communication barriers.

Some companies have experimented with flat structures, where there are very few or no managers between leaders and staff. The idea is to empower personnel by reducing the need for managers to tell people what to do. For example, I recently spoke to the leader of an IT firm who manages more than a hundred people with no middle managers. Teams come together for different projects, and they organize themselves.

This approach works for many companies, especially if they adopt it from the beginning, the company hires for this type of environment, and their goal is innovation. These flatter structures make sense for technology companies that seek disruption.

Not all companies can afford to remove all organizational labels and managers. As a real estate development company, we need more structure. Our workflows are sequential—we begin by finding a plot of land. From there, we design the building, obtain the permits for its construction, build it, sell or lease it, and then manage it. A completely flat structure would lead to chaos for us.

Even so, I have tried to integrate as much of this idea as possible into our organization. While this is difficult, a good first step can be finding a middle ground. While having some managers, you can still create empowered teams within different departments. For example, we have no middle managers, and each group organizes itself to achieve its goals.

We have relied on technology to make our business flatter and more fluid by removing parts of the work that can easily be automated. For example, we eliminated reconciliations between systems and took down barriers to communication.

If you decide to create a flatter structure, beware that hierarchy may be hidden within teams. Even if you succeed in removing it in upper management, you may find, as I have, that the groups may not follow the same pattern. Try to disseminate the idea of horizontality throughout the entire company.

A flatter organization lets you spread more skills across the entire company. For instance, instead of having a research and development team, you can design the company so that those skills and talents are a part of every area of your business.

In this type of structure, the teams become more autonomous because they can take control of all the responsibilities that contribute to how they build their final product. Information moves faster, and your team can make decisions immediately. Additionally, knowledge is accumulated in the right places. Each department starts to develop policies and best practices that improve the overall company.

Tailor Accordingly

Deciding which tasks belong in which department is not always easy. Some responsibilities can fit in with more than one category. In this case, you can build the function around an individual or team's strengths.

A company's overall structure will benefit if it is flexible enough to allow for occasional movements to improve the entire system. If the organizational configuration is strong enough, it can withstand small shifts in function and experiments with unorthodox ideas.

Be Wary of Barriers to Innovation

Functional organizations work best with only one primary type of product. If a company diversifies, it might consider another configuration, such as Divisional or Matrix, to respond more quickly and effectively to changing conditions.

These types of organizations are challenged by the barriers to communication that may emerge between different departments. If a company chooses a Divisional configuration with separate business units that work independently, it can end up with two HR departments as silos. In a Functional organization, HR is managed by one single department, and all the best practices and knowledge are accumulated in one place.

A company may not be able to remain in a Functional configuration forever. If the company has only one product with a longer development cycle, then the different departments in a Functional company can interact and create products efficiently and at scale. If there is more than one product, with a shorter time to market and wide product variety and customization, then a Functional organization may not be able to fulfill its mandate and innovate as quickly. Sooner or later, the company may need to evolve into another type of configuration, such as a Divisional structure.[25]

For All Organizations

Lateral Communication

Horizontal communication between departments promotes the free flow of information while preventing silos from forming. One way to achieve this is by adopting a Matrix organization.

When a matrix does not seem to be the answer, softer approaches can encourage horizontal linkages. Lateral integration across teams is essential even before reaching the point where a Divisional or Matrix structure might be a better choice.

These types of linkages can include task forces as well as cross-functional teams. Other initiatives are annual planning meetings, company-wide systems and communications, and cross-functional recurrent meetings.[26]

A company-wide management system or company-wide meetings are initiatives for lateral collaboration that can encourage communication across departments in a Functional or Divisional organization.

When interdepartmental coordination is necessary, managers will[27] naturally seek out others to work through any pressing challenges. Teams can also self-organize spontaneously within companies. These are grassroots, informal processes, and they arise as people work together across areas. As more communication happens, information is shared more freely.[28] When this occurs, company leaders can simply stand back and allow the organic organization to evolve on its own.

A team will become more horizontal if people get to know each other and learn to work better together and rely on each other. In company-wide meetings, everyone comes together to discuss the company's future direction. Cross-departmental projects are also rich opportunities for interaction.

When people understand the work that others do, a collective sense of responsibility emerges. People share the same strategies, goals, and language and fully recognize what each one does.[29] This enables collaboration to develop more readily.

Moving into a more collaborative structure takes time, and changes to a company's culture are better assimilated if you make them in small increments.

We have been trying to promote these lateral linkages via company-wide events. Every quarter, we bring the entire company together and celebrate birthdays. One of the most memorable events we had recently was celebrating all those whose birthday was in the third quarter of the year. It turns out a disproportionate amount of people had birthdays around those dates.

Our Corporate team bought a piñata, something we only do traditionally for children. Everybody hit the piñata. As soon as candy hit the ground, somebody would swoop in and pick it up. It was fun, and we laughed so hard as we played in a way we had not done in the past. The event's cost was negligible yet impactful.

Cross-Functional Teams

Decision-making used to be reserved for a few executives in an organization. Traditional vertical structures assumed they alone had the necessary knowledge to make decisions. If you hope to benefit from the entire organization's wisdom, decision-making should also occur via other committees and teams.

A cross-functional team brings together expertise such as IT, finance, engineering, marketing, and management to work on a challenge or project. Cross-functional teams include members from each of the different functions who come together for a purpose, for example, to implement a new product.

Permanent, cross-functional teams have been drivers for innovation in Functional organizations. These groups often report to executive management and not through their functional departments. An example would be a retail bank that brings together professionals with legal, marketing, IT, and back-office experience to manage its customer service. The team works together permanently to give customers and small business owners a better customer service experience.

Committee-based decision-making is also helpful in hiring and managing teams. In hiring committees, different people form a group to select the best candidate for a job. If the group is diverse, it will make much better decisions than any one person alone.

These teams support a company's strategy and may give participants a new level of accountability.

In Matrix organizations, cross-functional teams can help take down silos. Silos tend to crop up and prevent information flow, especially in companies with processes that do not link the company across departments. By bringing the players together into one of these teams to work on the challenge, we can eliminate communication obstacles and facilitate a quicker solution.[30]

Define Your Structure Clearly

The demands faced by a rapidly growing business may change quickly. When the company's configuration no longer works, it is vital to move from one structure to the next without remaining in a state of limbo between types of structures. Even during times of transition, taking longer than necessary in a Frankenstein-like amalgamation of arrangements will only make growth awkward.

If you have decided on a Matrix structure, do it thoroughly. Matrix configurations come with their own set of challenges. Try to avoid dotted-line reporting that is unclear and may lead to confusion. Instead, favor full-line reporting lines that everyone understands and can see clearly.[31]

We experienced an in-between phase at my company that lasted longer than needed. When we needed to move from a Simple configuration into the initial stages of a Functional organization, we stayed too long in a gray area where departments and their responsibilities were not clearly defined.

This phase created many problems. Sometimes, we did not have someone with clear responsibility for particular operations. This problem occurred in our legal department: our Corporate department managed some deeds and legal documents, and Properties managed others. As a result, we did not maintain an organized archive. Fortunately, we never lost anything, but it could undoubtedly have happened.

Our organization continues to change. At the moment, we have produced only one type of product, buildings, which take about a year to develop and 18 months to build. A Functional organization is working well for us. As we grow and add new business lines, a Divisional or Matrix organization might be a better fit for our future strategy.

Start Slowly

Start with your chosen configuration and, as slowly and simply as possible, add on elements. If you decide to implement a Matrix configuration, start small and lean.[32]

Similarly, if you choose to move into a Functional organization, add the minimum number of departments initially. By gradually adding on the pieces, you can fine-tune the ideal amount by splitting a department into two, for instance, and increasing the depth of responsibilities they have.

Transparency

Any organization will operate more smoothly if you eliminate unnecessary barriers to the free flow of information. In *How Google Works*, the authors say the job of an effective leader is to ensure information is shared and then to optimize how it flows through the company. In their view, Google "defaults to open" in all circumstances and shares almost everything (except information that it cannot legally disseminate) with its employees.

During their weekly, company-wide meetings, they present new product information that would be kept confidential in other companies. Google trusts its employees with key information, and they honor the confidence the company places in them.[33]

Each employee needs to have access to all the data she requires to perform her best work. Besides personal information held in the Human Resources department and competitive and confidential information in accounting, it helps to remove barriers between employees and the company's data.

In a company where information has not flowed as smoothly, it will take time to identify obstacles and eliminate them. It is impossible to immediately find all the impediments to the flow of information and instantly demolish them. Finding them is not easy, and weakening the current structure of the company could be a disaster. It is better to experiment and make progress while ensuring the company's character remains strong as it moves in the desired direction.[34]

I have found that unexpected boundaries keep cropping up. For instance, I have administrator-level access to our virtual document server. We have organized our documents to make sharing between team members as easy as possible. Once you get access to a folder, you can see all the materials within it. We designed our folder organization so their owners can share the entire folder with the new person, and he will have access to everything needed to do his job.

Inevitably, others from a different department will need access to some of the information. I used to get notifications every time someone shared one of the company's folders, so I could see that people often shared only one subfolder or a document, even if the person receiving the information might in the future need access to the rest of the files in that folder.

If a company's structure is not set up to maximize information sharing, boundaries will keep showing up. Having clearly labeled folders by department and visibility through our virtual tool about who has access to any files has helped improve the flow of information.

Changes in the Team

When a strong employee leaves the company, especially a manager, it is an excellent opportunity to determine if your organizational structure can be improved. It frequently happens, especially in growth periods, that people accumulate responsibilities that are not necessarily adequately structured around the company's current lines of reporting. Yet, because someone is already there, it is easier not to make changes. When that person leaves the company, it is an opportunity to refine your processes.

This type of transition can also be a chance to shake the tree of responsibilities. Sometimes, when a key employee leaves, I entirely restructure a department to make sure that responsibilities are more precise.

As an example, one of our managers left to pursue a master's degree. She was our first employee at Celaque, so she did a little bit of everything when she started. She managed our leases, helped oversee the design process for our first building, and even handled some accounting.

As we grew, we also developed a full accounting department and a team specializing in our buildings' designs, our Developments department. Our Properties manager had kept some functions such as obtaining building permits and new plot acquisitions, which belonged more naturally in Developments. When she left, we took the opportunity to streamline Properties, which made both departments run more smoothly.

Islands in Your Structure

As we strengthen Celaque, we make sure every operation is within the jurisdiction of one of the departments and is part of that group's systems and processes. Each department has its procedures and cross-functional processes and uses the same company-wide systems. When we decide to improve a process or add a new operation, having everything in its place makes adding one more item more efficient.

As we worked on Celaque's organizational structure, I kept discovering islands of roles and responsibilities that operated independently of the departments. Work was getting done, so there were no mistakes that drew attention to how we had organized the workflow.

At some level, these workflows could have stayed the way they did because they worked. But these "islands" resided outside the company's established functional areas, and they often had no manager responsible for them. That meant that if a problem occurred, it might not be detected immediately, and no one would be in place to solve it.

Also, inevitably in these islands, parallel processes had been developed that did not harness the company's already-existing systems and procedures, and additional effort was required.

When a company is close to its inception, these islands crop up when it is growing and work is more flexible, and before everything is together as an integrated organization.

You will often discover more displaced tasks than you initially imagined, and they are surprisingly resilient. These activities have come to be conducted outside the company's macro processes and are, therefore, independent of the procedures and systems you have implemented company-wide.

For example, one island I discovered had to do with the way we manage our properties. When a tenant vacates a unit, it is repaired and cleaned under the Properties team's supervision before a new tenant arrives. This arrangement makes sense because Properties is responsible for the units. But the Properties team did not have an engineer to verify that we had executed all repairs for the right cost. They relied on a member of the board of directors, who is also an engineer, to review the expenses.

Our Developments department handles construction and engineering, and its team of engineers and architects could easily handle the unit remodels. As our volume increased, it made more sense for Developments to take over the repair and cleaning. The remodeling of units had not fallen under Developments, so we had developed a spreadsheet-based system to manage purchase orders and construction budgets. It was inefficient because we were not harnessing our existing software to manage budgeting and construction, causing a loss to the team's energy and time at a company-wide level.

We decided to structure it differently. Whenever a tenant leaves, Properties alerts Developments, which draws up and approves a budget. Developments enters the purchase orders for the needed materials into our system, where they are approved. And finally, Developments supervises to be sure the units are in pristine condition.

A company's organizational structure is never finished. We also started to rely on the support from our Developments team for maintenance projects in the buildings we manage. On our first apartment building, Astria, we developed outdoor spaces for our clients on the rooftop terrace level, including a children's playground, a pet area, and barbecues. Some of these spaces included wood details. After a year of use, the wood became cracked, and the varnish started to peel.

When Properties came across this problem, the team did not have the contacts or expertise with this type of material. Furthermore, if they solved the problem independently without getting back to Developments, the team that had designed the furniture in the first place would not be learning from our mistakes for future buildings.

Once you finish working on one part of the structure, there is always something else. We must always consider change, and the structure itself can continually be improved. As you move islands from being handled independently to the broader company structure, you will strengthen the organization.

KEY TAKEAWAYS

- Create a solid foundation for your Heptagram-based company by defining the structural organization that will work best for it.
- Be prepared to improve your current configuration and evolve from one type of structure to the next when the time comes.
- In a Functional organization, take the time to make sure you have the right departments for your company and that the roles and responsibilities are clear within each one. Integrate entire processes within departments and functions as much as possible. This practice will give the work more meaning and will also create ownership.
- Remove unnecessary layers of management to make your organization as flat as possible to better respond to the changes.
- Find ways to integrate the organization laterally so that people communicate across divisions and functions. Cross-functional teams are a great way to take the company's strengths and harness them for better decision-making and innovation.
- When moving from one type of configuration to the next, start slowly but move decisively into the new structure. Do not stay in a middle ground because this will create confusion.
- Encourage the free flow of information between all the different parts of the company—it will improve decision-making.
- Always keep improving: take advantage of changes in your team to enhance your company's organizational structure and be on the lookout for workflows that develop outside the company's set infrastructure.

Two

Processes

> It's another paradox that management and planning require both chaos and order, and your job is to understand when one versus the other is the right course.
>
> – Linda Hill

Once a company's ideal organizational structure has been identified, the next step is creating the firm's processes, which, along with its information systems, define how work is executed in a company.

Processes that have been successfully set up and programmed into software ensure that everything runs smoothly and on time. Companies that have created significant business processes are better suited to deal with complexity.[35] They spend less time fixing problems that they could have prevented. And there is more time to respond to real-time challenges, projects, and new ideas.

The Heptagram model proposes the implementation of processes as the second pillar of business design. Along with the foundational structure, you need to think about how operations and workflows will navigate that structure's channels to deliver products and achieve results.

PROCESSES IN A NEW COMPANY

Processes are one of the most fundamental tools needed to organize a company. By setting up actions that occur consistently to achieve the company's objectives, your business will produce the results you want.

Having set workflows leads to consistency, but it is also a platform that will ensure the best results as you grow.

If you are starting a business, you will quickly discover that its operations are much more complicated than anything that can reside in any one person's mind. As your company grows, you will also realize that you cannot do all the work yourself, and at that point, you might hire someone to whom you can delegate part of the work. As the work increases, you will employ more people, and soon these people need to be organized and synchronized.

Not every company has set workflows. In some organizations, someone trains employees, and they perform their duties according to the parameters and the feedback they receive. When employees begin working in a company with no procedures, they develop their methods for getting the work done on time, which is not necessarily good or bad. However, if an employee is not trained comprehensively, there will be gaps in understanding, resulting in mistakes.

If you have not mapped procedures, it is unclear if the required steps have been executed consistently. Mistakes begin to occur. You may first notice that something important does not get done. For instance, a proposal that needed to be delivered to a client was not sent. When these types of things occur, you might spend more time putting out unnecessary fires than operating efficiently and thinking strategically.

The procedures you design will provide more organization, efficiency, and accountability for the work that your company needs to accomplish every day. At first, they address where you are at the moment. Yet, as the company becomes more and more complex, they become even more critical because procedures determine how work is executed through the company across functions.

Before the company can adequately respond to a complex and changing world, it must regularly execute basic operations with expected results.

DEFINING PROCESSES

A process is a set of tasks within a company that, together, accomplish a goal. It is a chain of events that leads a project from start to finish.

Processes can be strategic, operational, or administrative, and they follow a hierarchy. For each process, you may have a sub-process.[36] Therefore, each procedure is composed of actions that can be laid out on your to-do list so that you and your team can easily accomplish them as part of your daily work. These tasks can have due dates and will include detailed descriptions.

Processes include activities that you can assign to individual employees, across locations, and using various systems. They can cross departments, functions, and even companies, and they evolve with the company and are interconnected. Processes are how organizations coordinate the work of several departments, and they can be challenging to manage.[37]

Business processes are predictable and recurrent. They take place frequently, and the team working on them understands and is responsible for them. With time, they can become more automated and sophisticated.[38]

Most firms have a payroll process. Each month someone is responsible for making deposits or writing checks. This person likely has a reminder pop up on his calendar to not forget to make the payments.

Instead of relying on memory or calendar notifications, you can set up payroll as a process. First, create a diagram of how you are currently handling payroll and lay out the tasks that make up the workflow. The payroll process can be scheduled for the date on which you pay, say the 25th of the month, with the title "Payroll," indicating the tasks necessary to pay employees. The first task or step refers to a spreadsheet with each employee's payments and deductions. The person who manages payroll verifies the amounts he will pay against the spreadsheet for the current month and then writes the checks.

The process would show up automatically each month on the person's to-do list as follows:

Payroll
- Refer to Payroll spreadsheet for amounts to be paid
- Write checks
- Obtain signature
- Distribute checks

This reminder unburdens him from having to remember to pay everyone on time, and you will have generated a process that can grow with the firm.

To start paying employees via direct deposit, you modify the process to include that detail. You may also have someone who reviews payroll and monthly bonuses. The new steps now look like this:

Payroll

- Refer to Payroll spreadsheet for amounts to be paid
- Verify that the direct deposit amount is correct
- Calculate monthly bonus
- Notify manager for approval

This process now has built within it a level of review, and not only will payroll go out on time, but the manager will also review it to ensure it is correct.

In this simple version, the entire payroll process and its tasks are laid out with a single due date. This workflow describes the type of payroll process that a startup with only a few employees would have. As the company grows and becomes more intricate, you will probably have to break up these procedures to accommodate more tasks with different due dates and assignations.

I did not realize just how much work a company does every day until I started cataloging everything we do. Even if your company already has set workflows, it is a worthwhile investment to compile and analyze them, making any necessary changes. Processes are recurrent, so if one activity is inefficient, its effect is multiplicative, and the waste of time is replicated every time someone executes it.

Once you have mapped an organization's business processes and designed them to work together, the company will operate like a beautiful symphony. You will spend less time wondering about possible missing pieces and more time foreseeing future problems and thinking about strategy and innovating.

BENEFITS OF PROCESS IMPLEMENTATION

Companies always benefit when their business operations are streamlined. Implementing processes will cause your business to improve in many ways.

Greater Efficiency

One of the significant timewasters each day is being interrupted and forced to take care of unrelated tasks. Processes can help streamline those interruptions and organize aggregated tasks into groups. When an entire transaction is clustered, no time is wasted going from one activity to the next. Processes establish set times for accomplishing each task.

When I managed the sales team at Alianza, I was often asked how much space we had left or how many units we had sold. Sometimes, I could not answer because I did not have a set process for reviewing reports. When I began studying our key information, I realized I did not have the best reports available, which I later created.

I also had not organized my schedule. I would go over the reports at random times. When I was asked again about space and units sold, I found that my information was not up to date. Not having this information was embarrassing, and I had to find a solution.

To stay up to date, I needed to review the information every two to three days, and once I started using the reports consistently, I was able to reduce the reviews to once a week. I created a process whereby I aggregated everything related to sales. I was only doing it on certain days instead of reviewing the information when the thought crossed my mind.

The benefit of doing this type of review was, first, that it streamlined my effort into one sitting, saving time, and second, it ensured that I was reviewing the documents as often as necessary.

Better Organization

Processes also trigger the development of routines and positive habits. These practices help each person organize their time more.

When a behavior becomes automatic, it becomes a habit—our brain stores habits in our basal ganglia, one of the primitive parts of the brain. Once the brain saves a pattern, we no longer have to think in such a detailed way about doing this behavior. It acts similarly to breathing and is involuntary. Our mind is then free to stop thinking about how we walk or perform a monthly cash reconciliation. The habit liberates mental space to reflect on company strategy or new products.[39]

Routines provide a structured guideline for how we spend our days. Once a person develops routines organized around corresponding workflows, her schedule becomes more predictable.

Suppose that on Thursday mornings, Tom writes checks and organizes the payments that need to go out in the next week. If somebody tries to schedule a meeting with him on a Thursday morning, Tom knows that will not work because that is when he makes payments, and Tom's process guarantees that he will complete all payments on time. Tom's week is set up in a pattern so he can schedule the meeting for another time when he is available.

A trickle-down effect of Tom's process for payments will occur, and other people will start organizing themselves accordingly. If, for instance, payments go out only on Tuesdays, suppliers will stop calling to find out when checks are ready, and they will start to show up on Tuesdays. External vendors and suppliers will shape their routines around your team. This type of behavior can save time and money.

The processes' design will ideally consider the entire company and include all the main operational tasks to fit carefully together like a completed puzzle. Set workflows have the most impact when, through them, you can coordinate work across functions. When the team works within designed and scheduled processes, operations will run smoothly with a lower likelihood of missing actions or mistakes.

These gaps tend to occur when one person thinks somebody else is responsible for a critical deliverable. As soon as we spot these issues, we quickly assign the tasks to a team and document them in procedures. When everybody is clear about everybody else's responsibilities, no work will be lost.

At Celaque, we construct buildings that we sell or lease and then later manage. In the initial phases of construction, we negotiate the prices for all the building materials we will use. We then buy the supplies we need. The purchasing function crosses over a few departments: buildings require significant capital expenditures, and more than one team is involved. Procedures are vital for keeping everyone coordinated.

Three teams work together to negotiate the prices for the supplies we use, ensuring that we purchase the items at the agreed-upon price, receive the right number of articles, have adequately accounted for our inventory, and have accurately recorded all purchasing transactions. We have developed processes that tie all these actions together. These procedures ensure accuracy and synchronize each of the team's daily activities.

Everything that is recurrent is laid out and documented so that once each team member has received thorough training, they can practically run them themselves.

Ownership

Having set responsibilities is especially helpful when a new person joins the team. When we implemented processes, we reduced our onboarding time; the training period is now shorter than in the past, and the new person takes ownership of her responsibilities sooner.

We have also assigned processes by role. If one person moves into another position and someone else takes over from the original person, we simply select all the role's procedures and reassign them.

When each team member no longer spends valuable time wondering if everything is getting done or worrying about solving preventable problems, she will have time to think about and take ownership of her entire job. Organizing tasks also leaves more room for improvement because team members can find ways to innovate on their workflow and the results they achieve.

At Celaque, each person owns his work and is on the lookout for improvements that can be made. To support our teams, we created a process modification request form they can use when they need to modify or update processes.

The person requesting the modification assigns the form automatically to our processes team, which responds as promptly as possible to make our process modification workflow seamless.

More Accuracy

One of the most important benefits of implementing processes is reducing costly and painful mistakes that can trigger a cascade of adverse effects.

The description of each process will ideally explain everything that needs to be done for that specific task. If each critical step is documented, there will be fewer oversights. Errors are often costly— whether you must pay fines or repeat work to fix a mistake. They can also take a toll on morale.

Imagine a company that has not adequately implemented set business workflows. Now imagine it is busy with a significant system implementation, and its accounting team did not start the company's fiscal process on time.

The team eventually prepares the documentation, but there is not enough time to properly analyze and review its tax filing. An extra week would have been enough to find the best tax strategy for the firm. With no time left, and to avoid late fees, the accounting team decides to submit the information as it is.

Without a reminder to start preparing tax documentation on time, mistakes can occur. The quick process probably caused losses because the team did not have time to discover the laws' best application to ensure an optimum tax rate for the company.

It is easier to handle your procedures digitally because they can be programmed into the future, and you can track how your company is operating. The software can generate a recurrent notification when an action related to a process needs to start.

At Celaque, we use project management software to save all our procedures. The software will also record the details of routine, daily work. We found that it has been worth the investment of documenting everything and uploading it into a platform that will organize our work. As the firm faces new requirements, its processes can be updated to ensure they work better all the time.

Effective Time Management

Processes can help you automate your company's work. Automation allows the organization to eliminate steps and execute operations faster.

Once processes are laid out, executed at predictable intervals, and when they are repeated numerous times, they become automatic because they are recurrent and not haphazard.

When you design processes by analyzing the company's overarching operations, you can also cut out duplicate tasks and redundancies that naturally occur when growth is organic. As I implemented set workflows at our firm, I found different timewasters, such as two people executing the same task or tasks that took longer than necessary because they included unnecessary steps.

Inefficient ways of operating are natural, especially when a company is growing. The priority is to get the work done, and sometimes the way the company performs is not optimal. Process implementation can streamline these workflows for efficiency.

Better Results

Processes can help you deliver your products consistently and on time. Dependable procedures result in customers who will come back because they know they can count on the same results from you.

This consistency can extend to financial statements and welcome kits for your clients. Whatever you deliver as a company can go out on time and consistently. Not only will your clients be pleased, but so will your suppliers and investors.

The processes for a large company will be complicated. They will include different departments and assignees and may span a day or a few months. They will require more details and training. But the basic concept is simple—creating a set of steps that need to be taken regularly to ensure quality.

Data and Tracking

Once you have added business procedures to a process management platform, it will provide data and track the different activities and show how often your team performs them. Your system will help you analyze how well the procedures are working.

As you are sifting through the data, you may find errors in how you configured the company's workflows. You may also notice that a person or team is overloaded and consistently behind. The reports may point to a need to hire another person on that team.

You may also notice other ways your company's processes can be improved. During one of our procedure revisions, we saw that they were not formatted well. This review prompted us to improve how we were formatting and organizing the procedures. We examined all our processes, revised the content, and standardized the formatting to make it consistent across departments.

Our guidelines for processes included not only how we presented the content but how the procedures were categorized. We also reviewed how we managed the dates so that the timing between different team members was staggered and a person's schedule did not become overbooked on any given day or week.

Additionally, we clearly labeled where each of the tasks fit in the larger scheme. For example, we identified them by team and showed what action came before it and what job came after, helping our teams to collaborate better.

Cultural Shift

With the help of designed business processes, your team will start working together for the same goal and towards achieving the same results.

When goals are shared, tasks are more visible, execution is more effortless, and individual responsibilities are more explicit. Over time, processes become part of your company's culture because everybody sees how essential they are. People collaborate more smoothly, and everything gets done on time.

IMPLEMENTING PROCESSES IN YOUR COMPANY

Processes will help you grow your business. Setting up workflows for an entire company takes a significant investment of time and effort. To get started, study the daily tasks you and the rest of the company perform, and then start implementing your procedures. I recommend beginning with the most critical areas, where an error can have significant consequences. You can work through each department until you document and configure every significant procedure.

Ideally, you will develop a plan to design and implement your company's processes fully. However, if that is not possible, any improvement will be noticeable. Implementing set procedures or redesigning the workflows for your firm's most vital areas will make an enormous difference in time management and productivity.

We have divided our types of processes into those that occur recurrently and those that follow a sequence. Recurrent processes are those that are repeated the same way, every certain amount of time.

These processes can be daily, weekly, monthly, quarterly, and so on. Examples include calculating yearly bonuses and weekly approval of outgoing checks. They are anything that is done again and again, at fixed intervals.

Sequential processes describe a set of steps that someone takes every time a specific event occurs. A sequential process is a checklist. Hiring a new person follows a sequential process with critical steps that follow a set order. To start the process, you post the available position and receive resumes. You may send out a questionnaire, and you then perform telephone interviews. Next, you do an in-person interview, and finally, select a candidate and negotiate the offer.

The tasks are logical and easy to remember, and each primary step has detailed sub-steps. Without a checklist, it is easy to forget something. In the previous example, it is useful to include the list of places where you advertise the new position. If this subtask is not present, you will need to think back to remember the resources you previously used each time you want to hire someone. What you create is a live checklist that is continuously updated.

As a real estate development company, we are always selling properties, and each time we sell a unit, several actions must take place to complete the transaction.

Before we had documented our procedures, whenever someone overlooked a crucial action, it was left undone until we discovered the mistake.

We were handling about ten to twenty sales transactions a month, and the risk of error was too grave; we needed to organize our process. We decided to create a comprehensive listing to ensure that all steps were covered. We then shared our deal-closing list on our project management software and collaborated on the same steps for every single closing.

Compiling all the actions in the closing process was an achievement. The more steps we wrote down, the more we realized we were missing. As we collected all the information, we recognized that we did not have a proper procedure for closing a sale before this exercise.

We chronicled all the steps, along with dates in which they had to be completed and by whom. Here is a summarized excerpt of the list:

- Create and review the contract
- Print out an invoice
- Obtain signatures and deposit, hand out the invoice
- Give deposit to our accounting team
- File contract
- Close sale on the system
- Make sure to update the system database with final closing details

We tried to make our list as succinct as possible. If there are too many steps, they are less likely to be followed. Additionally, one person does not perform all the steps: Sales is in charge of updating the system, whereas our accounting team has to take care of the funds and the transactions. The salesperson activates the checklist and assigns the tasks to the different departments once we have closed a sale.

Even today, the list is a work in progress. Every time we discover an error, we ask: What can we do to make sure this does not happen again? Every quarter, on average, we add a new step or adjust an existing one. Changes in regulations have also prompted modifications to our checklist.

To store and maintain our checklist, we use project management software. The software allows us to create templates that we can duplicate each time they are needed. We have carefully designed each model and stored it with a description, dates, and assignees. When we anticipate a new closing, the salesperson activates the templates, and everyone immediately receives their assigned tasks.

Sales are time-sensitive, and closing a transaction must be done quickly and accurately. Everybody knows the timeliness involved in closing sales, and the minute anybody receives a sales-related task, that activity becomes that person's immediate priority.

The templates are adaptable. If a sale takes longer than anticipated due to the client leaving on a trip and delaying the contract signage, for example, they can quickly shift the due dates. The descriptions can also be modified if there is a special request by the client: they can add comments, and if necessary, several people can collaborate on a single task. Once they have completed the work, the checklists are archived for future reference.

We have been using our checklist system for a few years now. The beauty of the templates is that we do not worry anymore about forgetting an important task. We have documented every step, so everything we need to do gets accomplished. All significant documentation is complete and adequately stored.

Please go to www.pamelaayuso.com/heptagram-bonus and download our monthly accounting close process to see more details of another of our main procedures.

PROCESS IMPLEMENTATION BEST PRACTICES

Process implementation will vary from company to company. What follows are some of the "best practices" I have found as we have implemented our processes in Celaque.

1. Diagram Your Workflows

I recommend diagramming as a great way to visualize your process automation. A diagram is a visual representation of how work gets accomplished in your company. You use different symbols to show operations and information flows. You would start by listing each of your business's significant functions: accounting, logistics, sales, marketing, and research and development, among others.

Then you can select one, divide it into subcategories, and diagram how each process currently operates. Accounting, for example, can be divided into subcategories, including expense and income management or financial reporting and auditing. Include in the diagram details such as who is responsible for each task and what other departments it goes through for approval.

The goal is to find hidden inefficiencies and timewasters and question if there is a better way for work to flow. You might be surprised by how obvious specific problems are once you lay them out visually. You might spot redundancies or work that was not executed, or the operation might be too convoluted. You may find workflows that can occur more efficiently and with less wasted time. For instance:

Inefficient Processes

- One person may be taking the same action as someone else without the other person's knowledge, and as a result, they duplicate the work.

- One person may be repeating a task every day of the week, even though that is unnecessary. Instead, she can execute it as needed, but no earlier, reducing wasted time.

Potential Errors

- Lack of supervision in essential areas: Critical reports and processes, such as financial statements, are best reviewed by more than one person to ensure accuracy.

- Lack of reconciliation can occur between systems and reports, especially with legacy systems or when using spreadsheets. Ideally, to avoid reconciling information, all reports should be generated from one central database of company information. At times, the company's budget may not allow for a system with that capability, and you will need to reconcile relevant documents. For example, you may need a process for checking inventory availability against sold items so that quantities and descriptions match.

- Tasks that someone needs to perform that do not show up on anybody's to-do list: When creating a diagram of how work is flowing in your company, you may find that some functions are not being done or are not being performed often enough. This problem will have to be addressed by assigning the activity to a team member and specifying how often the team needs to do it.

Heavy Workloads

- Some people's jobs are full of essential tasks, while others on the team have lighter responsibilities: Diagramming your current workflows can help you detect where workloads are uneven and correct that accordingly.

Lengthy Processes

- Too much bureaucracy can slow down the company and affect its bottom line. A diagram will indicate where bottlenecks are so they can be trimmed down or redesigned.

- Your company procedures may take longer than necessary. This delay may occur because of a lack of communication or no connection to the result. The person may not know the importance of that specific deliverable.

- Deliverables go out on a specific day because they always have, even if a different time would be more efficient. Analyzing your current processes will show the team what timing will make your work effective.

As you diagram, look for and analyze ways that you can streamline your current workflow. The processes team can work with the person responsible for the task to evaluate and improve it together. Some questions you can ask are the following. You can print this list at www.pamelaayuso.com/heptagram-bonus:

- Is there a better way to perform this process?
- Does the current structure contain risks, and what mistakes could occur?
- What is the worst-case scenario given the present configuration?
- What could I add at the end to ensure that we have reconciled everything and we have minimized mistakes?
- What steps can I eliminate to simplify the process as much as possible?
- How can the team choreograph their processes like a dance?
- How can tasks be distributed among the team so everyone's workload is balanced?

These are good questions to ask for any area of your company. After completing the first few, you may want to go back and improve your original diagrams because the goal is to understand the tasks involved as well as possible.

2. Design Your Company Processes

The next step is to create a diagram of how each task should work. The workflows you design should be as simple and fluid as possible. The OHIO principle, which stands for "Only Handle It Once," is beneficial to ensure items are only worked on completely at set intervals and not in bits and pieces.

The idea is to group related tasks, schedule a recurrent time, and work on them only at that allotted time. Instead of jumping from one job to the next, you can do everything related to one area in one sitting and only work on the task at hand at that point and continue at it until it is complete. The OHIO principle will greatly increase your company's efficiency.

If you apply the OHIO principle to your company's weekly accounting review, you will view all the reports at the same time every week. Instead of cycling through different statements at different times throughout the week, you can make a list of all the critical metrics/ reports, such as accounts receivable, accounts payable, and cash flow, and review them in one sitting.

Classify and Organize Your Processes

Once your diagram shows a broad sketch of the processes in their ideal configuration, you are now ready to identify and classify them. List them all and see how they tie together. Group them by areas.

At Celaque, we have grouped all of our processes by categories. This type of organization makes processes easier to find and manage. We have identified administrative work as one of the primary areas in our Sales department. Here we include everything related to paperwork, such as digitally sent proposals and signed contracts and updating any reports. All this work is grouped in one process and performed at one time only to save time.

Before implementing them, try laying out the procedures you have listed to see how they fit with one another. We usually map out all tasks on a calendar to verify that workloads are consistent. We compare to make sure the due dates of the process are orchestrated between team members, as in the case of one person depending on the other to complete a procedure.

Assign Complete Responsibilities

Sometimes a process becomes fragmented when one person takes care of one piece of the project while the next person takes care of another step. A way around this is to designate one person to complete the entire process and another to review it. A bonus is that responsibilities are then entirely clear, and you have added a level of review.

Seeing the whole process from beginning to end can be motivating to your team. According to a *Harvard Business Review* paper by Ayelet Fishbach, when people start working for a goal, they usually begin enthusiastically, and then towards the middle, they lose that drive. If the person cannot see the result, the loss of energy in the middle of a project may be accentuated. Fishbach quotes one study where observant

Jews were to light candles on eight successive days, beginning the first night with one and adding another each night. The participants were more likely to light the candle on the first and final nights but not on the other six nights in between.[40]

Seeing the impact of a process is more motivating than merely being a cog in the company's wheels. Employees are inspired when they connect their actions to the final impact—for example, by meeting customers who benefit from their work.[41] This experience will transform their work from an abstract concept into a specific appreciation of how they contribute to other people's lives.[42]

When an employee is entirely responsible for a process, he will know he has to answer for the results and must make the right decisions to guarantee those outcomes. Exercising judgment on the job can increase a feeling of competence and effectiveness. This autonomy at work includes structuring and organizing one's tasks, impacting decisions, and utilizing one's skills to best suit the organization.[43]

When designing processes, the challenge lies in balancing the company's best overall workflow while also leaving space for independent decision-making and autonomy. One crucial step is ensuring that the group views processes as their tool for maintaining work quality and timing. Departments will ideally have the freedom to modify procedures as they adapt them to how the group operates.

Design Them to Be Durable and Flexible

Companies and people are constantly evolving, and procedures must do so as well. If you do not design the processes to be resilient, they will be too rigid and either become a burden or eventually collapse.

To make processes perpetually relevant, they need to be able to evolve. They need to be emergent to adapt to the changes that occur around them while also being robust to maintain their purpose. The trick is balancing flexibility and durability. Here are some strategies we have used at Celaque:

First, each person oversees her processes. When someone enters our company, one of the essential parts of training is how procedures work and that they belong to each team and individual. As a person starts to rely more on them, processes become tools that support them in performing the role, rather than an imposition. By taking ownership, each person will adapt them as becomes necessary.

We also make sure they can be quickly reassigned or moved. The software you use will ideally allow quick changes to the assignee, dates, and descriptions. If a person is away on vacation or leave, he can easily reassign the processes to another person or move them to a different date.

Finally, the less bureaucracy there is for workflow changes, the better. Processes are the programming for how a company operates, so they should be altered carefully.

Your processes should be as long as they need to be but no longer than that. As Atul Gawande explains in his book *The Checklist Manifesto: How to Get Things Right,* not all checklists are made equal. Boeing's flight operations group issues more than one hundred lists a year.

Dan Boorman, a veteran pilot at Boeing, says there are useful checklists and bad ones. "Bad checklists are vague and imprecise. They are too long; they are hard to use; they are impractical... [They] try to spell out every single step. They turn people's brains off rather than turning them on. Good checklists, on the other hand, are precise. They are efficient, to the point, and easy to use even in the most difficult situations. They do not try to spell out everything—a checklist cannot fly a plane. Instead, they provide reminders of only the most critical and important steps—the ones that even the highly skilled professionals using them could miss. Good checklists are, above all, practical."[44]

Not every action a company takes will be part of a process. There must be plenty of room to work with the unpredictable because we work in complex environments, and you cannot script a great deal of what happens at work.

Processes should balance checklists with space for independent thought and collaboration. The lists ensure that you accomplish all the necessary steps to achieve the company's primary objectives and omit nothing, freeing up space for creativity and entrepreneurship.

Create Time Savers

As you are designing workflows, make sure they are as efficient as possible. To save time, find ways to cut out steps from your teams' workflows. For instance, instead of downloading information from a platform, have it sent via email, for example, to be available when needed.

Automating your office's procedures brings numerous benefits. These sometimes small, time-saving ideas will add up over time and make your workflow smoother. Every bit of energy and time you save allows space for growth and improved development.

Creating templates and lists for documents that you and your team regularly utilize are great ways to streamline work. Some examples of models are:

- By creating a client proposal template with the information that goes in all proposals, you only have to customize it whenever you or your team must send a document to a client.
- If you send every new client a welcome message, you can program the message into your software to automatically send after you close a sale.
- Create spreadsheets your teams will use every time they need to execute a process. You can refer to the documents or templates in your procedures to become a part of the workflow.

There are other ways to create timesavers. Simple notifications can make a significant difference. Our company produces sales that are large in size but smaller in volume, so everybody on our client-support team receives a message every time there is a sale. This notification has saved us considerable time by simultaneously keeping everyone informed.

Consistency

Spend time thinking about how you wish to format your processes and the documents that support your procedures. Consistent guidelines for document configuration can have an enormous impact on workflow and productivity.

The less time we spend trying to understand how something works, the more time we can focus on the content itself. Consistent formatting also helps us work more quickly because we know and identify the general guidelines. If you multiply this concept throughout an organization, you will save valuable time, which you and your team can use to improve quality overall.

There are many advantages to using consistent guidelines for your documents, processes, and customized input screens. You will spend less time identifying what the document is trying to say because you know where to find the information you need. Also, if the same formatting is used in every spreadsheet, users will instinctively know what to expect. Each person will be able to quickly find a title and recognize the main takeaways from the document.

With consistent guidelines, you can ensure all your documents and reports will be better because nothing will be missing, and you will be able to find errors more easily. If something is not in line with the general format, it will jump out.

When configuring your processes, aim to standardize titles, list formats, and any codes you may use to identify them. You can organize these by function, department, and user. The more consistently your processes are formatted, the more the user will focus on the content.

Our configuration guidelines for procedures include how we present the content itself and how the processes are categorized. Each action has a header that classifies it by department and process. The objective of this categorization is to make each procedure identifiable by simply looking at the header.

We developed guidelines for the list formats we use within procedures, how we refer to external documents, what spacing we use, and what headers we employ. A consistent format helps the user quickly understand and recognize the flow of a process.

3. Implement and Review

As your company grows, invest in the most sophisticated software to automate workflows that your budget will allow. Every second you save per transaction adds up to minutes and, ultimately, hours.

The software you use will help you manage all the information in your processes. You can program your information system so that your processes appear on the date they need to be executed. The software will also assign them to the responsible party. You can collaborate on processes as a team and update them as necessary.

If the software you use is easily customized, you can tweak it so it saves steps. Simple changes can improve how your team communicates and can also reduce errors. We often use request forms, one of our process management software's features. They are entirely customizable, so we can add any field, decide to make it mandatory, and add attachments. At Celaque, we use them for expense and negotiation approvals.

These forms have been beneficial, especially with expense approvals. Sometimes we must make large purchases, and to ensure that we have all done our due diligence, we receive quotes from more than one supplier, and we also make sure we are within budget. To that end, we have added several fields that gather all the necessary information. Using the request forms, we confirm that the expense makes sense, making approving a purchase easy.

Once you have implemented your processes, the next essential step is to follow up carefully to ensure everything flows smoothly. You will likely have to make adjustments based on the feedback you receive from the primary users. Look out for incomplete procedures, duplicated items, problems with timing, and misunderstandings. Please visit www.pamelaayuso.com/heptagram-bonus to download a list to check your processes.

- Incomplete processes may show up during implementation, which lack critical details.

- You may discover that parts of the process are duplicated.

- Once users start working with the procedures and have a clear sense of the work involved, it can become easier to detect that one person has a heavier workload at the beginning of the week or month and lighter at other times.

- Misunderstandings will occur if your procedures lack clarity. It is best to document processes with enough detail for even new team members to execute them properly.

- On the other hand, some operations may be too long and need to be summarized or divided into two parts.

4. Modify and Polish

Modify and polish your processes until they shine like jewels. Keep enhancing them, as operations are ever-changing and procedures are never permanent.

Moving to a process-based model is iterative, and the procedures in the firm will be continuously updated and improved as the team provides feedback. You learn about what works best for your situation. Once you have a good base, you can quickly execute modifications due to workflow, personnel, or timing changes.

Processes document how you have completed tasks in the past, how to avoid previous mistakes, and how to improve work quality. If processes remain static as the company's best rendition of history, learning and adapting to the future will be difficult. Again, procedures must attain equilibrium between "learning from the past and experimenting with and adapting to the future, and between rules and constraints versus freedom and flexibility."[45] They need to adapt and respond to the future.

Continue to simplify and automate. If you keep looking, fixing, and streamlining, your improvements will add up over time, and the opportunities are endless. As technology progresses, you can upgrade how you do things ranging from simple time management enhancements to updating to software that better integrates your company's different departments.

5. Process Maintenance

Processes require maintenance. Employees move to different roles or leave the company, how you operate changes, and the authorities modify regulations. For processes to remain relevant, a business must plan and prepare for change.

When we underwent our process revamp, we did so because we realized that we needed to provide greater transparency so that users could see how the entire process flowed from beginning to end. Users could more easily see how each action was related to the goals of the company.

This finding led to an overhaul of every process and a review of each department's overall workflow. While examining the content in our processes, we discovered things that no longer applied, such as the names of past employees or teams. When we finished, we added a procedure for ensuring that our processes are always up to date.

6. Process Review

An effective review procedure will be thorough. Once you have compiled all the information, you can organize it by team, function, frequency, and assignee.

It is essential to have a master file that includes all the major processes, timing, and responsible parties. With a database of every procedure, you can compare its information against the master file, see if anything has changed, and determine the reason for any alterations.

This master file can point to any issues, such as missing information or room for improvements like shifts in dates or better categorization. It will provide the basis for discussion when the processes team meets with each of the departments.

The idea is that each team devotes time exclusively to the review. I recommend doing this as frequently as necessary, perhaps once or twice a year. The teams will go over each process to ensure it is still applicable and decide if anything can be improved or designed better.

Preferably, the processes team will go over everything with each user. The user may not see how their role fits into the company's larger picture. Similarly, the processes team will not have the operational context that the users have. Both perspectives can come together to achieve the best possible outcome.

The time spent reviewing processes can be a training opportunity for new team members and a chance for leaders to see the big picture of their daily work. Finally, each team learns how processes work and can make the necessary improvements. Simple adjustments can smooth out the number of tasks at hand and help improve workflows overall.

In the end, make the necessary adjustments and update the processes and the master file. Ensure that you remove all old or irrelevant information and that everything is classified correctly. Performing this maintenance work prevents significant errors from accumulating and will help catch any urgent changes in time.

You may find emerging processes that you wish to document. Please visit www.pamelaayuso.com/heptagram-bonus to download additional material to help you record new procedures.

Fixing Problems in Your Processes

Once you have implemented processes, you will still sometimes run into problems. Perhaps a newsletter did not go out on time, or a report was missing information. It pays to figure out what happened and solve the issue for the future—processes are often a valuable resource for long-term solutions.

It is vital to discover the root of the mistake. A useful technique is the Five Whys approach. Initially developed for the Toyota Company, the Five Whys helps you discover the actual cause of any problem by asking why it happened, then why it happened, and so forth until you get to the fifth why.[46]

For the Five Whys to be effective, you must first make sure your problem statements are accurate and that your answers are honest.[47] You may also need to determine who had ownership of the subject area through questions such as: Who is currently responsible? Who should be accountable? Do not be surprised if you learn no one was responsible, and that's why the problem occurred. Timing can also be the source of the issue. Ask: When should it have happened? How often should it be done?

Postmortems, in which the entire team gathers after it has completed a project to discuss what can be improved next time, can also be useful, especially when there is a set process for postmortems. Performing a postmortem involves the exploration of past failures, something people naturally tend to avoid. A structured process will help overcome their hesitancy.

One way to conduct a postmortem review is to create a survey to gather information from the project's participants. Survey questions can address whether the team properly established lines of responsibility and whether meetings were productive. Postmortems also involve debriefing meetings, metrics analyses, collectively developing a hypothesis about what went wrong, elaborating on obstacles faced, and proposing solutions to prevent future mistakes.

To permanently address failures, you can correct missing items in the company procedures. Last but not least, postmortems' results should be communicated throughout the company.[48]

Communicate and Implement Changes

Everybody involved must understand why the problem occurred and know how it is getting fixed. Communication is a step toward making sure the problem does not happen again.

Problems will always happen. How you and your team react to them will make the most significant difference in your company. As you invest more and more in your processes, they will get better, more comprehensive, and they will make your company more adept at responding to current events.

Even with all the investment of time and effort that processes represent, I do not know how we could have managed to grow without them. Our work as real estate developers is full of details, which may be small but vital.

For years, I wrote reminders to myself at night or on weekends of items missing from our processes to prevent these types of errors. As we improved, we reduced the number of mistakes. It turns out there is a point when operations become more stable, and mistakes become fewer and far between, or as Lucy Maud Montgomery put it in *Anne of Green Gables*:

"But have you ever noticed one encouraging thing about me, Marilla? I never make the same mistake twice."

"I don't know as that's much benefit when you're always making new ones."

"Oh, don't you see, Marilla? There must be a limit to the mistakes one person can make, and when I get to the end of them, then I'll be through with them. That's a very comforting thought."

Processes have been our key to developing consistency in how we operate. The investment has paid off in providing something that, to me, matters the most: peace of mind.

KEY TAKEAWAYS

- Processes are one of the most fundamental tools needed to organize a company.
- You can set up processes for every significant workflow in your company.
- Investing the time in creating set procedures for your company will result in greater efficiency because similar tasks are grouped. People on your team will waste less time going from one activity to the next.
- Processes help people create routines that organize their work and the schedules of others around them.
- Because responsibilities are clear, each person can take more ownership of the work.
- Procedures help you save time because you can automate your work, and they provide better results because they ensure consistency.
- Setting up workflows requires studying the daily tasks you and the rest of the company perform.
- Procedures can occur recurrently or be triggered by an event. Recurrent processes are those that are repeated the same way, at regular intervals. Sequential processes describe a set of steps that someone takes every time a specific event occurs.
- Diagrams of how work gets accomplished in your company will help you uncover inefficient processes, potential errors, and heavy workloads.
- Visualize how you want work to flow in your company and design your procedures to align with that ideal. As you design, remember the OHIO principle and try to group related tasks.
- Also, classify and organize your processes by significant areas so that they are easy to find and understand.
- In your design, try to assign full processes and not fragments so that responsibilities are clearer.
- Create durable and flexible procedures that will be able to evolve with your company.
- Find ways to save time as you craft your procedures and make sure that they are consistently formatted.

- Implement your procedures and make sure you follow up to ensure they are working well.
- Processes require maintenance, and they can always be improved. Make sure you set time and resources aside to take care of what you have implemented.

Three

Information Systems

> The beginning is the most important part of the work.
>
> – Plato

In the Heptagram model, process design and information systems work together. Everything you envisioned in terms of the type of structure your company needs and how processes should be implemented will crystalize in how you customize the technology that will help you achieve your goals.

A few years ago, Celaque embarked on its most significant information system implementation: NetSuite, an Enterprise Resource Planning (ERP) system. It took six very intense months to become operational. The full process lasted a year because we discovered problems we needed to resolve as we started using our new software. The information system interacted with all the departments of the company, and bringing it online affected everybody.

Before implementing an ERP system, we had basic accounting software. While it was a sound system for a startup, we quickly realized we had outgrown it. We now needed ERP software, a system that links a company's transactions from the origin to the end, from purchasing to accounting and into sales. We wanted an information system that would take a purchase order from creation to the approval process to the billing function. With an ERP system, you can only pay the bill if the underlying purchase order has been approved, instituting more control and checks across the system.

Due to its complexity, the ERP required that we work with consultants to help us program it. They oversaw setting up the fundamental workflow and modules within the system in a way that made sense for our business. With the help of our implementation consultants, we developed a plan with timelines and detailed steps for how we were going to mold the ERP system to fit our needs.

We started working alongside the consultants in each of our departments. We were involved throughout the implementation process, and we asked many questions. Their roadmap helped us get the software ready to work at a fundamental level. However, it was challenging to verify that the consultants were programming what we needed and wanted. We could not see the final product until the end, and we did not have much time for modifications.

Once they completed their work, the system was functional, but the programming only partly fulfilled our expectations. We knew it could do much more for us, and any further action by the consultants was over our budget. Consultants have no way of knowing as much about a business as its people. We had to get deeply involved in setting up the software for ourselves, and as a result, we ended up with a much better work product.

This stage was the most intensive part of the process. We were trying to learn how to use the system and simultaneously become operational. I created a cross-functional team within our company, and we started working on it. We improved the functionality of each screen we used to capture information and the fields in each one. We added dozens of fields for each of our specialized operations.

We also created all the reports we needed. We started by looking at all the spreadsheets we used and worked with each department within the company. Accounting is the backbone of the system, so we began in this area. Accounting was also where we produced the most spreadsheets.

Many of the reports were native to the system, and we did not have to make any adjustments. For example, the system generates all the financial statements. We created financial reports, fiscal and supporting schedules, and reports that showed all essential transactions and their approvals.

Once everything was ready for activation, our next step was transitioning from our two previous solutions: Zoho Books, our accounting software, and Zoho CRM, a Customer Relations Management (CRM) system. Although our ERP addresses more of our needs, it is always difficult to move from the familiar to the unfamiliar. With that in mind, we gave ourselves two deadlines: by March of that year, we would stop using the accounting software, and by June, we would leave our CRM.

Both transitions proved to be complicated. Although our consultants helped us create opening balances in our accounting module, we still had to complete the missing information. Our initial deadline was going to be March, and we were going to start to input transactions beginning that same month. Once we started, however, our accounting team decided to include the entire year's operations, so they also recreated January and February in the information system.

The new schedule represented a lot more work, but having all the information in the system from the beginning of the year allowed us to pull complete reports by the year's end. As a result, our external audit process at the end of the year was much more straightforward than it had ever been before. Taking that extra time was worthwhile.

Moving from our CRM to our ERP software involved fewer steps. The major transition required moving our contacts into our new system and setting a deadline for our switch. A week in, I realized the team was using the new system but keeping our old CRM as a backup. It was understandable, given the newness of the transition, but we ultimately decided to move entirely onto our ERP system and remove access to the old system.

Next, we focused on refining everything we had programmed. One of our significant crusades was eliminating all our spreadsheets. Through years of working with spreadsheets, I have found that they are prone to recording and amplifying errors. The need to reconcile documents to compensate for this problem is too time-consuming.

We gradually got rid of almost all our former spreadsheets, one by one. In our Properties department, we handled our portfolio primarily by using three to four spreadsheets. In Finance, all our accounting support was also processed via dozens of worksheets. The Sales department managed all our availability in spreadsheets. By generating reports directly from our ERP software, we eliminated most of the spreadsheets in all the departments.

We also spent much time perfecting workflows for processes in each of the areas. For example, we purchase our inventory for construction using purchase orders. Previously, we had never worked with software that included this mechanism. It took us a few months to get the workflow just right within the ERP. One person inputs the purchase order, and another approves it. We experimented with a couple of approval methods until we finally discovered that the information system had a native approval process that worked the best.

We continue to make our ERP system as tailored to our needs as possible, but the rewards from all our hard work are already immense. Our information is accurate and available on-demand, something we never had in the past. I realize though, that system enhancement is a never-ending process because our business will continue to evolve, and the information system must change with it.

THE IMPORTANCE OF INFORMATION SYSTEMS

Information systems support complex and automated workflows; they are the mechanisms a company uses to program its overall business processes. Teams within a company must collaborate, and workflows must move from one person to another, from one unit to the next. When a company becomes more complex, its processes do as well.

The interdependence necessary for departments and teams to share and coordinate with each other over business procedures can be programmed into information systems.[49] An information system gathers, processes, saves, and disseminates information to its stakeholders and supports its business operations. It helps managers analyze and problem-solve, which can undergird managerial decision-making.[50]

As a tool to hold overall business processes, information systems have many advantages. They save time, minimize errors, improve quality, and make progress easier to track. Furthermore, information systems speed up communication within the team, with customers, and other stakeholders.[51] Research has shown that companies using their information technology to support their business processes correctly are more competitive.[52]

Technology can solve the challenges companies are facing. Every company is different, and some software is more adaptable than others. The right overall solution gives your company the results it needs. More often than not, the right solution that will provide your company the results it needs is a combination of information systems to fill in the necessary gaps.

In the past, the most viable options available to smaller organizations were lesser-quality software systems that were shared via a local server and maintained by an outside IT person. Most of these firms would either choose those solutions or kept everything on spreadsheets and shared documents on an internal server. It was a frustrating and outdated way to work.

Our journey was like that of many other small companies. Here is a short account of the problems we faced with their corresponding solutions.

STORIES IN SOFTWARE IMPLEMENTATION

Accounting and Sales

We started experimenting with a local, server-based accounting software solution when we first invested in an information system. We quickly found out that it was too limited and archaic. The software handled almost nothing, and it turned out to be a wasted investment. When Cloud software became affordable soon after that, we found we could feasibly move our information online. Cloud software was easy to implement, giving us complete visibility over all our data. It was what I had been seeking.

Our priority was accounting because we did not have an adequate mechanism to record all our transactions. We were a small company and used spreadsheets to record all our operations and then give them to an outside accountant. Often, the information was not complete, and we did not have financial statements on demand. We also could not search for prior transactions. We had outgrown our technology.

We needed an information system that could do the basics of:

- Issuing invoices to our customers and recording collections
- Recording bills to be paid and applying payments
- Reconciling our bank accounts
- Creating financial statements

We did not have a large budget, and the option that made the most sense was Zoho Books. Implementing the software took some time: we had to develop templates for our invoices and figure out how we would use each of its features. As we learned to use the new technology, we also sought to improve our accounting process. This accounting system was a big part of that evolution because it enhanced the accuracy of our recordkeeping.

At the same time, our sales team needed a CRM system to record all interactions with our customers. We wanted to keep track of all our calls and conversations, register our sales transactions, and maintain an updated inventory record. We needed something inexpensive yet comprehensive, and we selected Zoho CRM.

Before we had that CRM, we kept our information on spreadsheets, and we had to sort them continuously. On one particularly infamous spreadsheet named "Contacts," we maintained information for all potential clients, with additional columns for status and comments. We sorted through it to see who we needed to call and who was no longer interested in buying from us. The changes were not always recorded or up to date, and sometimes we lost a sale. It was a nightmare.

Our new CRM system immensely improved our sales process. Here are some of the things we were able to do:

- Search for a client and see all sales transactions
- Manage deals already in progress
- Pull reports on accumulated data
- Have a record of all the sales and returns

Our CRM software did not have a function that would let us record our inventory, so we kept a separate spreadsheet for our list. It also did not integrate well with our accounting information system—we could only import contacts. Our invoicing process was very manual, as our sales information did not flow into our accounting program.

A few years later, we were ready for more advanced functions. Our accounting system could only process elemental transactions, such as bills and invoices, and produced fixed customer statements, accounting reports, and financial statements. We are real estate developers, and our industry has quirks that do not fit into standard business models. We not only sell properties, but we lease as well. Our manufacturing process varies from building to building and sometimes from apartment type to apartment type.

We managed our purchasing via spreadsheets, our accounting via Zoho Books, and our sales via Zoho CRM. To operate successfully, we had to reconcile between reports and upload data from one information system to another. It was too inefficient—we would need to manage all our company's transactions using only one comprehensive solution moving forward.

We purchase materials we use to develop a building that we then sell or lease; this overarching process had to be tied together. If we wanted to join purchasing with accounting and sales using a streamlined information system, we required ERP software. Many options are available, and some even specialize in real estate development. They provide automation, accuracy, personalization, and flexibility.

I quickly realized that an ERP system designed specifically for real estate developers was beyond our budget. We decided instead on software that could be adapted to a variety of industries, with the intent of modifying it to fit our needs. That is when we implemented our ERP.

Project Management

The next major information system we implemented was software for project management to handle our processes. We had managed our operations informally; each person knew or was trained in her responsibilities and kept her tasks on a notebook or planner. Nothing was organized or adequately structured. We would solve problems as they arose.

For projects or to solve issues, I would meet with each person every few days to find out about progress on specific items. Too often, I discovered a miscommunication within the team about the task itself or the time frame. If the other person or I had not recorded the assignment for some reason, we could easily forget it — never to be seen again.

We needed a tool that would oversee procedures for the firm and allow us to work better collaboratively. I noticed that we could easily solve many of the issues we encountered. They were recurrent because we had not adequately discovered our processes or structured them within an information system.

I visualized a company-wide platform that would list all our processes along with their due dates. They would show up recurrently on each person's daily to-do list. Nothing would get lost, and we would be able to follow our progress clearly.

I eventually selected Wrike as a project management tool and a firm-wide organizational information system to manage our business processes. We were able to increase our productivity as a team because of greater transparency and accountability. This software also allowed us to collaborate as a team on tasks, including sharing documents and pictures. Plus, we had a reliable mechanism for keeping track of personal and group assignments.

RESEARCHING SOFTWARE

The first step in selecting an information system is evaluating what you need it to do for you. Be sure to involve other key players within the firm so that the solution is responsive to all your requirements. Some of the topics to consider are as follows. You can download this checklist at www.pamelaayuso.com/heptagram-bonus.

- **Budget**: Your number of users determines the cost. Some information systems allow an unlimited number of users and have an insignificant cost per year; others are affordable only by large corporations. Be on the lookout for implementation costs, which are sometimes required.

- **Types of access**: Not all your users will need full access to all features. For example, with accounting software, only a few users need full administrative access. If you are implementing a document storage software, you may require read-only access for some users and full access for others.

- **Security features**: Look for control features, such as approvals, audit trails, and notifications, among others, and know what you need.

- **Reports**: Ensure the information system provides the data you need, including reports that aggregate the information in its databases.

- **Currencies and languages**: If you have operations in different countries, you may need the flexibility of multiple currencies or languages.

- **Integrations**: Make sure your software can integrate with other software you may be using. Some examples include being able to upload documents from your virtual storage software to your project management solution.

I recommend researching various information systems and setting up a chart that helps you compare your requirements against what each software you test offers. I still have not found any information system in my budget that fulfills 100 percent of my needs. As you research, keep an open mind because you may discover new needs once you see what is available on the market.

Once you have narrowed your choices to two or three, take advantage of any free trial periods to test each solution and of the software company's sales representatives to answer any questions or to demonstrate step-by-step how to use the program. Some information system features not obvious from the company's literature will be identified by trying out the product. You may also discover that some software solutions are awkward to use, while others are easier and offer more flexibility than you expected.

After the testing phase, you can start the process of selecting the information system. I like to create groups of stakeholders and testers to find the preferred solution and how it could work at my company. I have found that the more involved the stakeholders are from the beginning, the better the implementation will be because they will take ownership and will also find ways to improve the information system as it becomes a part of our operations.

Sometimes, after the research and testing process, you may not have found one information system that fulfills all your requirements. Or perhaps one is perfect, but it is not within your budget at the moment. Depending on how urgent your needs are, it might be best to wait because implementing a new program is a significant investment of time and money.

IMPLEMENT YOUR SOFTWARE

You may have a team in place to implement your new software or the resources to hire someone—or, as was right for me, you may be doing it on your own. I do not have a degree in technology, but luckily, technology is increasingly user-friendly, especially with simple, entry-level programs. For more complicated endeavors, having a professional at hand is the ideal situation.

Creating a Plan

To begin implementation and to save time, form a plan for your project's overall deployment. Consider who will configure the information system, how you will move your data from what you were using before, how you will train your team, and how user adoption will occur once the information system is live. To save money, you can have everything ready to begin working with your software as soon as you buy the license(s) after the trial period.

One of the necessary steps is to determine how you want the infrastructure of the program to work. Be sure to study the available controls, how information flows, and how different modules in the information system operate. Some of the more basic software solutions are easy to configure with intuitive features that you can customize to your needs.

Sometimes system implementations are too complicated, and you need to work with consultants as we did with our ERP software. After we purchased the program license, the external team interviewed us to learn how we worked and what we needed by department. Then, they presented a plan for how they would implement each area and started programming; finally, they trained us.

Configuring the Software

With a plan in hand, you can start to configure the software. As you set up the information system, you will determine how the work will flow in the software. I view this as a highly creative part of the process because you will resolve how that part of the company will operate. How a system is configured will have to mirror how work flows typically, but there is inevitably innovation, and it is a great place to make improvements in company operation.

After setting up the system (e.g., controls, fields, input screens, reports), you will upload all the necessary data to the software. If you have been using another platform, you may have to download your current files to upload them to the new information system.

In some cases, you may have to recreate information, although this may be difficult. If doing so is too costly for you, you can upload information only after a specific date. If your cutoff is at the beginning of the current year, upload only the current year's information and archive earlier data for future access. You may also be able to retain limited access to your old information system to store archival material.

After the system is operational, the next phase is to train your teams. Fortunately, this is easier as software interfaces are becoming more intuitive. The information systems' Help sections and Forums have documentation and suggestions for bringing your users onboard.

Depending on the complexity of the program, you may need to implement formal training plans. As you create new ways of using the software, you can enrich these plans. These training programs will be useful in the future when you are hiring new team members.

As you conduct customized training on using the software and its features, the goal is to get them as comfortable as possible. The more personalized the training is, the better. It is best to organize training by team, and if possible, to have the leader of each group conduct it. Each team can then handle questions or comments about the software as they arise.

Once everybody is trained, it is time to begin using the new software. Consider in what order users, teams, or departments will start, what will happen to prior information systems, and if there will be an overlap while the new information system is coming online. Instead of buying all the licenses immediately, you can save costs by staggering the start dates.

Wasted time can be one of the biggest problems in these types of implementations. To avoid unnecessary delays, set deadlines for the completion of the different steps in your plan.

Obtaining Feedback

Because user feedback is vital to the information system's success and adoption, I recommend setting up an evaluation process as your teams start working with the software. Through it, you can make changes as they arise and take into account all assessments. Your business, technology solutions, and processes will be better because of it.

You can always make improvements to ensure that your solution provides what you need, and the feedback you receive will be crucial to refining anything that needs polishing. Information system enhancement is a never-ending process because your business will continue to evolve, and your information technology must change with it. Some improvements to take into consideration are as follows. Please download this checklist at www.pamelaayuso.com/heptagram-bonus.

- Most information systems allow you to add customized fields to the screens that will help you collect the data you need to create your reports.
- Creating new and better reports to aggregate the information you need for decision-making.
- Improve the information system's workflows by adjusting how the information moves (what steps to take first and what actions should follow) within the program to mirror how you work in your firm more closely.
- Create dashboards you can check for a quick snapshot of your department or company.

Software implementation requires a significant money and time investment. However, if you have chosen your information system wisely, your productivity will reach new levels, your data will be organized, and you will be able to perform tasks that you could not in the past.

Continuous Improvement

Information systems can grow with you, especially if they are customizable. After you have implemented your software, you can always improve it to make it more efficient and useful for your company.

After our lengthy ERP implementation, we found that what we had could improve how the software worked. We continued to refine and enhance the system. We spent much time perfecting workflows for processes, such as processing purchase orders for our inventory to ensure they flowed smoothly and efficiently.

We also programmed our system to be visually consistent. The information systems you use in your company, such as CRM or ERP software, may be customizable. We set up all the screens in our information systems to follow the same layout. At the top of each screen, we place the entity the record belongs to, like the customer or supplier. Then, if there is a value associated with the same file, we have placed it on the top right-hand corner.

For every screen, we follow similar guidelines so that users will look for entities, values, and other recurrent fields in the same places. We also defined general guidelines like the number of columns in each screen, how titles are formatted, and the order and grouping styles of information.

Some information systems come with tools and platforms that allow businesses to alter the software and adapt it to a company's needs more closely. The ability to customize is an additional benefit of transitioning to more advanced solutions. Our ERP, for example, has a platform that allows companies and developers to add to it and modify it. Once we implemented it and it managed all our principal transactions, we decided to develop enhancements to automate further and eliminate errors in our operations.

We selected the most important areas to us and which would have the highest impact on our time.

Inventory Availability

Our first enhancement was programming to manage sales inventory availability better. As a real estate company, we had to store our portfolio inventory in a separate database from our ERP sales module. Whenever we sold or leased a unit, we would have to update our inventory availability manually. We needed a solution that would update our sales transaction and our portfolio availability simultaneously.

We programmed workflows that tied both modules together:

- When we enter the item number (e.g., an apartment's number), the item's description (housed in the inventory module) automatically fills in the sales module.
- When an opportunity closes (i.e., we complete a sale), the inventory module item is automatically marked as unavailable.
- When a lease expires the inventory item automatically changes to available.

This enhancement in availability has sped up our sales process and significantly reduced mistakes. We analyzed the new programming for a few months, and initially, it had a couple of errors, but we corrected them.

Invoicing

Our next priority was to produce recurrent invoices for the portfolio of properties we manage. We are responsible for billing rent and other fees to apartments or office space. The invoices have many moving parts, depending on the property; ours include monthly rent, late fees, and maintenance fees, and each of these items can vary and depend on different factors.

At one point, we managed a facility's accounting, sending out about 300 invoices monthly to the building complex owners and lessees. Compiling and distributing invoices initially took about two weeks per month. Although we were using accounting software at the time (Zoho Books) to send out the invoices and manage payments, we were still manually uploading the invoices one by one.

Then, we found a way to automate the process with templates and spreadsheets with formulas. Although this new solution saved us time, we needed something better. Because each month we must prepare hundreds of invoices for each of our customers, we wanted a solution that would automatically generate the invoices on the 25th of each month by pulling all the information from the client's screen. Creating this process was easier said than done because we needed to program the following variations (among others) into our invoices:

- Lease rate: This is the main item we are billing. The prices are different depending on the type of unit and its size.
- Late fees: If a payment is past due, late charges accrue.
- Taxes: Tax regulation varies by type of asset.
- Maintenance fees: We charge maintenance fees on some assets and not on others.

We tried to make the entire process automatic, but there were inevitable errors, mostly with the late fees, because there were too many details that we would have needed to include. In the end, we programmed a hybrid model where 90 percent of the process is automated, and the other 10 percent, including late fees, is uploaded and reviewed manually.

Ideally, an overall software solution will be seamless and straightforward. That is not always possible because the right program may not exist to solve all the issues you wish to address on the budget you desire. However, you can find a solution that will take care of most of your transactions. You can then add other solutions that will address additional issues. The goal is to build your most flawless software mix.

The technological landscape is continuously evolving, and solutions that will fulfill your company's needs may already be waiting for you. Sometimes it takes creativity to discover how to pull together new and disparate elements. Keep improving your overall software platform. You can always find ways to simplify, refine, and update your technology, and the more attention you give, the more your operations will be enriched.

KEY TAKEAWAYS

- Information systems support complex and automated workflows: they are the mechanisms a company uses to program its overall business processes. When a company becomes more complex, its operations do as well, and information systems will support this growth.

- Technology has many benefits. It saves time, reduces errors, improves quality, and makes progress easier to track. It also helps us communicate more quickly.

- As a company, you will need to craft an overall technology solution that works for you. You will likely need to work with more than one information system to solve all of your company's needs.

- To begin implementing your software, make a plan for how you wish to deploy it. With a plan in hand, you can start to set up the software. How a system is configured will have to mirror how work flows typically. There is inevitably innovation, and information systems are a great place to make improvements in company operations.

- You will have to determine how you want to manage your old data and how you want to train its new users.

- Because user feedback is vital to the information system's success and adoption, I recommend setting up an evaluation process as your teams start working with the software.
- Never view information systems as rigid frameworks; allow them to evolve.
- Information systems can grow with you, especially if they are customizable. You can keep improving them so that they evolve and help you operate smoothly and efficiently.

Four

Metrics

Once the first three pillars of Heptagram are in place, i.e., organizational structure, information systems, and processes, now is the time to measure your organization's performance. Metrics give you an overview of every vital part of your business's current state, and that tells you if it is achieving the desired outcomes. Parameters, such as your number of sales or projects in the pipeline, are the indicators that will show you where your company is headed.

I first saw the value of metrics when I started working in Sales. I wanted to learn about how the market was behaving and how I could respond to it better and sell more. I also wanted to measure how effective I was in my new job.

I started by counting the number of leads I was developing, the calls I was making, and the number of sales I closed. The more I learned about sales, the more questions I seemed to have. I knew I could answer them with the correct data, but I realized I needed to improve my indicators, so they included the information I wanted to have at my fingertips. I then developed other reports to try to find more information and gradually added more statistics.

These numbers started to give me an idea about the market trends for office space, and later, the residential segment. Once Alianza became the most significant competitor for office space in our city, the metrics we gathered showed us the limits of that market. There were only so many square meters that we could sell and lease in a year.

The numbers told us there was a threshold to how we could grow by building only office buildings—we could not fill the entire city with offices. We needed to move into new markets. That's when we decided to start constructing apartment buildings.

After we built apartments in three different buildings with Alianza and one with Celaque, we realized we had hit another ceiling. Our metrics and our market studies showed us that the demand for apartment buildings in the city's most central parts was not large enough to provide sufficient growth for the company. That led us to build more affordable housing in other central locations in the city.

Other indicators showed us that when people have confidence in the economy, they buy. If their trust is reversed, sales go down, and leasing goes up. This data convinced us to diversify into leasing, so we could always take advantage of different market cycles.

Ray Dalio, investor, hedge fund manager, and author, describes the value of measurement and metrics in his book, *Principles: Life and Work*. His advice is to develop statistics for the entire company. "Build great metrics. Metrics show how the machine is working by providing numbers and setting off alert lights in a dashboard. Metrics are an objective means of assessment, and they tend to have a favorable impact on productivity. If your metrics are good enough, you can gain such a complete and accurate view of what your people are doing and how well they are doing it that you can almost manage via the metrics alone."[53]

We started with sales metrics and then built them for the entire company. As Ray Dalio suggests, they have become an integral part of how we manage Celaque. Metrics lift the curtain, letting managers and team members learn more about how they are doing, how we are all doing, and whether we will meet our company's goals.

Company-wide indicators are a way to get a complete picture of its results and hard data on its leading drivers. The statistics will be unique to your company, although some main parameters apply to all companies, and others refer to specific industries. You can draw inspiration from others and learn from best practices. Metrics are best, however, when they are tailored specifically to how your company is working. They are most effective when they are your singular amalgamation of data.

BENEFITS

Key Performance Indicators (KPIs) are defined goals that you and your team want to reach. They help align each unit and the daily actions that are vital for achieving a company's objectives. Metrics measure how well everyone's activity is catalyzing those ultimate results.

As leaders, we articulate a company's strategy and hope our employees understand the role they play. Strategy tends to be very broad, and it is not always clear what a team can do to achieve its overall objectives. As everyone does their daily work, it is easy to lose sight of how accounting, IT, marketing, and product development go together—yet they all play critical roles in producing and selling a product.

Well-designed KPIs help bridge the goals to the actions, instilling in team members a sense that they are all working together towards the same purpose. Indicators can show everybody how all the work ties together and help everyone understand how they can gear their actions to the same result going forward. Also, you can use indicators to improve work performance because when everyone can see progress, it will motivate action.[54] The performance will become more consistent as metrics are measured from period to period.

Another benefit of implementing metrics is that they create ownership and enhance trust because the company relies on its team to choose the best path possible to reach its objectives. They empower teams and individuals. Leaders provide the company's general objectives, and then everybody takes the necessary actions to achieve the results. Finally, metrics help us learn.

DEFINITIONS

Not all indicators are the same, and some distinctions are useful. In his book, *Key Performance Indicators: Developing, Implementing, and Using Winning KPIs*, David Parmenter lists four types of metrics. The differences in concept are useful because choosing the right one will help you create the parameters your company needs.

Metrics are either results or performance indicators. You can compile them at a company level, which are the Key Results Indicators

(KRIs) or Key Performance Indicators (KPIs). Measuring at a team level provides Results Indicators (RIs) or Performance Indicators (PIs).

Results indicators, which may or may not be financial, report on the accumulation of one or more teams' actions. They are the outcomes, compiled monthly or quarterly, and therefore, do not provide daily in-progress information. This kind of measurement does not give you details. You might need to make changes before the results have become final. Some of the results indicators we measure at Celaque are the number of sales we have had in the last month or week and the vacancy rate in our property portfolio.

Performance indicators are the levers that create the outcomes the company is seeking. They are not financial. These metrics are linked to a team's or set of teams' performances, and these teams are responsible for them. They help the team see how well they are lining up with the company's strategy.[55]

One way to explain KPIs is by taking apart the words that make up this acronym. The term "Key" means it is vital for company operations. Not everything can be critical, so part of the metrics selection process involves identifying your company's most significant parameters.

Next is the company's "Performance," which is a measurement of the drivers that make the company move forward.[56] They need to improve performance, which can be measured, calibrated, and managed.[57]

Finally, "Indicators" pinpoint qualities we can quickly determine as desirable or undesirable. They are like a temperature gauge that can give a manager insight into the future results and help make decisions that will help us improve the likelihood of achieving the results we want.[58]

Useful KPIs, according to Harold Kerzner, in his book, *Key Performance Indicators,* "sit at the nexus of multiple interrelated processes that drive the organization. When activated, these KPIs create a ripple effect throughout the organization and produce stunning gains in performance. When an executive focuses on a single, powerful KPI, it creates a ripple effect throughout the organization and substantially changes the way an organization carries out its core operations."[59]

Examples of KPIs are late deliveries, which can be divided by manager; the number of initiatives implemented after a team satisfaction survey; the number of innovations planned for the next 30, 60, or 90 days; timely arrival and departure of airplanes; and significant projects running behind schedule.[60]

When we began making our list of metrics, we noted the numbers we thought we needed to monitor. We did not divide everything into results and drivers. Initially, we simply wanted to record the information. We have since refined these, and that led us to determine the main drivers of our company. What matters most is getting started and working at this until you find the right metrics for your company.

START FROM ZERO

Be careful not to rely simply on intuition when choosing parameters. This point is illustrated in Michael Lewis' *Moneyball* about how the Oakland Athletics team in California harnessed the power of statistics to assemble a highly successful baseball team. In the beginning, the baseball scouts used their experience and intuition, not statistical data, to measure how the team is doing.

Lewis described how teams primarily used a person's batting average to measure how good he was. But when the Oakland A's performed a statistical analysis, they found that a better predictor for scoring runs was how often the player got on first base. Their scouts began selecting new players that scored high on this measurement. An added advantage was that players graded solely by how often they got on first base were priced less expensively, and the Oakland A's were able to recruit several that no other team was focusing on.[61]

A problem with using intuition in choosing a metric is how marred the process can be by our cognitive biases, such as overconfidence, which causes us to think we know more than we do.[62] Using only our intuition will lead us to include parameters we believe are essential merely because we consider they are important, not because we have evidence supporting their significance.

Another cognitive bias that affects us is the "availability heuristic," a mental shortcut whereby we judge how often an event happens or an item's size based on how frequently similar instances or things come to mind because that is the most "available" information we have.[63] If we hear about a particular statistic often—from other businesses or within our own company—we might mistakenly assume it is crucial simply because we can quickly recall it.

Finally, we generally have an aversion to future losses, which seem more significant than the potential gains. We are biased to accept smaller, not more substantial changes. As business leaders, we prefer to stay with what we know rather than seeking changes in how we do business, which causes us to prefer maintaining the status quo, our current situation.[64] We, therefore, may be reluctant to drop metrics we are used to in favor of newer, more effective ones.

Ray Dalio proposes metrics that provide you with the necessary information to know the company is producing the outcome you expect. Picture what your company needs to know and how you can respond to that with numbers—and build the indicators that provide them to you.[65]

Metrics should measure cause and effect. To start, define what your company's main objective is. It will probably involve creating value (e.g., profitability or growth in assets under management). Next, find the key levers that make your company work and can take you there. Look first at the results you are working towards and identify key milestones to help the company reach those goals. In an article in the *Harvard Business Review*, Michael Mauboussin defines the best statistics as *persistent*, meaning they will produce similar outcomes at different times, and *predictive* in that they exhibit a causal effect for the desired result.[66]

This exercise takes some time and thought. It is essential to build metrics that work for your organization. Instead of focusing on what you already have, think of what you need. Start with parameters that you believe will lead you to the outcomes you desire and give you the information essential to running your business.

One way to find this information is by listing all the obvious answers and quantities you need to run your company: for example, how much cash do you have available at any given point? Consider what indicators will take your company to those results. Also, it may be beneficial to measure the events that could be the riskiest for the business. Develop numbers that will alert you before a significant problem such as low cash flow occurs.

Try to understand what levers drive the results you are seeking. For instance, if customer service is crucial for the outcome your company is seeking, focus on the actions your company must take to improve in this area. Some might include having a faster response time or more flexible conditions. If necessary, you can also measure the actions that can be broken into sub-steps to produce the desired indicators.[67]

These parameters should not be limited to the standard metrics, such as new prospects and sales pipelines, which may or may not be *predictive* and *persistent* for your company. They can also include the parameters that are crucial to your industry, and more specifically, to your company, such as innovative implementations within each of the company's teams. Some of these indicators may not be used by your competitors—they might be your special formula, the ones that make your company unique.

Initially, it is best to think about as many different perspectives and indicators as possible because, through creative metrics, you will see your company from a completely unexpected angle. With time, those indicators will change and evolve.

SELECT YOUR METRICS

Some of the indicators on your list may be financial, such as costs, while others are nonfinancial, such as customer service. It is essential to evaluate whether the nonfinancial metrics predict an outcome the company is seeking, so you can avoid measuring drivers based on intuition rather than data.[68]

Figuring out how many indicators you should have in your company can be confusing. David Parmenter has developed a 10/80/10 rule for organizations of more than 500 people to follow: they should have 10 KRIs, 80 RIs and PIs, and 10 KPIs. Smaller companies can reduce the number of RIs and PIs.[69]

After I determined at Celaque that we needed our own set of metrics, I launched a year-long project to define our company's leading drivers and results and compile them month after month. It took a year to arrive at a set of statistics that gave us the information we needed.

We started going department by department, imagining what the most important metrics were for each one. We worked with each team to develop the most critical parameters, and in some cases, what we came up with diverged from metrics we had predicted for that department. This analysis was valuable because we were creating indicators that fit with the company's current reality.

With our list of metrics in hand, we began finding ways we could procure the data monthly. Metrics are useless if they are not comparable and available consistently. We wanted our parameters to be company-wide, so we needed to compile them from widely different sources.

For instance, a construction safety company monitors the safety of our construction process and our buildings. They provide a monthly report of our safety indicators, and we use that to feed our company-wide data. We also use our property management system and website analysis sites to compile other information. Most of our data comes from our Enterprise Resource Planning software and is available on demand.

We started with that initial list in January, and every month, we discussed changes that we needed to make. Some metrics were not coming from the best sources, so we had to improve that. Other parameters turned out to be irrelevant.

We made changes every time we found something wrong, and the list grew, then shrank and grew again. We continue to iterate our list of company-wide indicators, which continues to evolve. Each of our teams has its metrics, and they refine them to make them more valuable.

Recently, I created a list of new results indicators: they are income streams in one of our departments, giving us a clear picture of their total value and letting us compare them from month to month. Some lines are blank because they represent projects we are launching soon. The blank lines show that nature abhors a vacuum, and I hope they will quickly be filled in with positive numbers. In any case, we have a clear understanding of how the revenue for that unit grows (or not) every month.

IMPLEMENTATION AND FEEDBACK

I recommend working with each of your teams to compile the master list of metrics to build the entire company dashboard. Each team's manager will use these statistics as they lead their departments and make decisions. These indicators will also give the group clarity around the results they can contribute to support the company's overall mission.

Some of the parameters may be already available; others may not exist or may have to be modified. If the metrics are not readily obtainable, you can create the reports to continue collecting them regularly. Sometimes your software may not produce the reports on-demand, and in this case, you can rely on tools like spreadsheets to compile the information. The data in these reports will aid in managing your company and where it is going next. They will show you how well the organization is achieving its goals and what vital levers can be improved to correct any wrong turns.

Additionally, make sure the metrics you compile are consistent. If the information you are gathering is not comparable because your systems are unable to produce it or you are relying on different sources each time, then you will not be able to draw accurate conclusions.[70]

Feedback from individual team members will let you know if the indicators reflect the team's reality or if you can represent the information better. Sometimes, the parameters may not provide value, or a team member may point out useful alternatives. Compare these suggestions across the teams and identify the best practices that can improve information across the organization.

Refining the indicators will produce the closest representation of Ray Dalio's metrics dashboard. Continuous improvement and enhancement are crucial, and the best set of parameters will be the most straightforward combination of numbers. When we implemented the use of metrics at Celaque, some of the indicators that appeared necessary at first no longer seem as relevant.

As we started using our dashboard more and more, we found other parameters that could be simplified or combined. In some cases, we compared two different indicators to show the relationship between the two. We added metrics where we needed them but tried to keep the minimum number of parameters possible. We found too much information to be overwhelming and hard to absorb.

ANALYZE THE INDICATORS

Metrics will show trends and patterns. One single parameter may be misleading, and determining trends[71] across a set of metrics is itself a skill. Once you have six months to a year of data, you will see patterns and learn how key parameters are developing.

You may find cycles in your sales, for example, that you did not know existed. Tendencies emerge in the metrics that indicate how your company, or even your industry, is evolving.

These indicators can show new growth opportunities. You may also measure where the results are improving or falling behind. This valuable knowledge will reveal worrying trends you can correct before it is too late. You can alter the company's direction in time so that improvement happens regularly and before significant problems occur.

We have used our metrics to take actions that help us save money. Our Developments team created a set of parameters to measure how well we were negotiating with our suppliers and to ensure we are obtaining the best prices and staying within budget. One of our most significant indicators is how much over or under budget we are for each project. Celaque's first project, Astria, had gone over budget, and we wanted to prevent that from happening again. Too late, we realized that we had budgeted too little for some line items, such as labor and interior decorations.

For our next project, Agalta, we created a better projection and found ways to save where we could. Our initial budget for Agalta turned out to be larger than we had expected. We analyzed in greater detail where we were spending money and found some construction items that we always purchased last-minute, which were not part of our initial contracts.

We could negotiate some of these items upfront, eliminating the need to purchase them during the construction process when the expenses were higher and harder to adjust. Through this analysis of our purchasing metrics, we saw how we could save in this area.

Our monitoring of each line item during our construction process led us to develop better indicators for line items that usually resulted in overages in our budget, like concrete and steel. We monitored world prices monthly for steel, and we tried to time our purchases with periods when prices were lower. And if we had to purchase steel when prices were above what we considered was average based on world prices, that information helped us renegotiate. With concrete, we used metrics to reduce waste to a minimum and lowered overall costs.

Metrics will also give you, as they did us, data on expectations versus reality. If you are measuring, for example, how long a project took compared to your initial forecast, you might find that the original plan was overly optimistic. In the future, it will help you set realistic goals and plan accordingly. Depending on how detailed your metrics were, you can identify key milestones to improve in future projects to get better results.

COMMUNICATE

Ideally, each team prepares its parameters instead of creating a department to do this for the entire company. This work will help everybody on the team see how well everything is going. Since the indicators result from their work, and they are responsible for putting them together, the team will have ownership of the process.

Analyzing the most important trends as a team—for instance, in a management team or a departmental meeting—will draw out more valuable information than if one or two managers view it alone. Different representatives from interconnected departments across the company will see things from other perspectives and provide valuable opinions on where the company is heading and what improvements you can make. There may be critical parts of your company that you are not measuring, and gaps can be identified in these meetings and remedied.

There will be KPIs that move your company. It is vital to communicate what metrics matter the most and to be sure everybody understands them. The more everybody knows what factors determine the company's success and the direction in which the company is going, the more everyone will work to achieve similar goals. A saying attributed to Peter Drucker reminds us: "If you can't measure it, you can't improve it." Unless everybody on the team is clear about the company's essential parameters, they will not have enough information to take necessary actions.

KEY TAKEAWAYS

- Metrics provide an overview of the current state of every vital part of your business. They are defined goals that you and your team want to reach, and they help align each unit with the daily actions that are vital for achieving a company's objectives.

- When designing the metrics that you will use, start from zero. Choose parameters that are real levers for your company and show a clear cause-and-effect relationship with its goals. Some of the parameters you select may be specific to your industry; others may be particular to your company culture.

- Selecting your metrics is only half the battle—making sure you can collect them consistently from the right sources is the other piece. The information must be coherent so that it is comparable.

- As you start working with your dashboard of metrics, you will find some are not valuable, or there are better ways to represent the information. Keep refining them so that they become as useful as possible in managing your company.

- As you compile the data, you will start to notice patterns and trends that will help you learn more about your company and take timely action.

Five

Trust

Those who trust us educate us.

– George Eliot

One of the challenges we face as company managers is infusing the company with a sense of trust. Organizations that inspire confidence run more smoothly, and trust also makes work more enjoyable.

From a human relationships standpoint, Trust is the main pillar of the Heptagram model. You could design a structure, processes, information systems, and metrics, but when you are working with human beings, trust is at the heart of the system.

When people are trusted, they produce better results. A traditional method for motivating employees is through external rewards, such as raises or perks. These benefits work, but they can also prompt undesired behavior that is tied to those incentives. Trust is different because it appeals to intrinsic motivations. It is linked to better performance and a commitment to the projects. In a trustworthy organization, people are more engaged in achieving the company's goals.

Part of trust is being vulnerable and putting ourselves in someone else's hands. Being vulnerable can be difficult, primarily because it is often easier to take matters into our own hands to accomplish what we want to achieve at the beginning of our careers. We may not be used to having to put our trust in someone else.

A trusting organization starts with the leader, who must be willing to go first. Trust involves putting oneself in situations that have no guarantees. Trust is a virtuous cycle. When one person trusts, the other reciprocates, and others will follow the example set forth by those who trust. As the company becomes more immersed in trust, performance will improve, and its overall environment will be more pleasant. Those who honor trust will be drawn to the organization's culture.

The best way to determine how trust will work for your organization is to experiment. Some things may work, and others may need to be tweaked. Nevertheless, greater autonomy and confidence will create a more engaged and dynamic organization, which will inevitably be more decentralized.

THE NEED TO DECENTRALIZE

When something needs a timely response in our rapidly changing world, there is rarely enough time to communicate the situation to company executives before a decision needs to be made and put into action. It is impossible to centralize all decision-making.

After we finish constructing a building at my company, we either sell or lease the units and then we manage the building once it is occupied. Issues can happen at any time. For example, one of our tenants decided to have a loud party on the rooftop terrace on a Saturday night, even though this was against our building regulations.

Our city is hilly, so noise on one terrace traveled to other houses and buildings around it. Someone in one of our neighboring buildings called the local authorities and asked them to shut down the party. The building manager is part of our Properties team. She immediately took control of the situation, mediating between the tenant and the authorities and avoiding a citation to our building and a fine. Later, she implemented a new measure to ensure that no loudspeakers were allowed outside.

One way to ensure that organizations are nimble is to push decision-making power to every part of the company, to the people dealing with vendors and customers. With the right team in place, each person can rely on the company's infrastructure to help them solve problems related to their work as they arise.

Creating greater trust in an organization may seem counterintuitive to the need for processes and structures, which are meant to minimize risk and errors. However, those tools exist to support the organization's people; they can wield the processes and company infrastructure to help them get their jobs done well.

Redundancy will occur. Actions may not be taken in the most effective way possible because the person may not have the full perspective of the company that an executive may have. But the positive effect of decentralizing will far outweigh any loss of efficiency.

As decision-making is increasingly decentralized, your organization will have greater resilience. More people will be able to deal with a greater variety of circumstances, so if one part of the company cannot work through a problem, another will. The entire company increases its adaptability.

Trust in business is based on newer psychological research about internal motivations and how they create better results than external motivators. In the past, companies looked to external rewards to promote productivity. Psychologist B. F. Skinner developed the theory of operant conditioning, which describes how external conditions can control behavior.

Recent research is moving away from external rewards. Intrinsically guided methods are based on the belief that humans have an innate motivation to grow and achieve. People will complete any tasks, including those considered boring, if they understand their importance.

The critical difference between these approaches is motivation. Carrot and stick methods will center on external rewards, and those focused on autonomy rest on internal motivation. Operant conditioning-based approaches work, but the incentive is not sustainable because it is not self-driven and may encourage undesirable behaviors such as cheating to achieve external targets.

Employees are happier and more productive in trusting environments. Two studies by Paul Baard of Fordham University, Edward Deci, and Richard Ryan of the University of Rochester, tested large U.S. banks. They discovered that employees who felt they had more autonomy and support from their managers were more satisfied with their work, improved their performance, and had lower anxiety levels.[72]

When employees accept and adopt company structures, such as policies and processes, making them a part of how they work, their work becomes meaningful. If employees view rules and procedures as imposed externally, they will desire external motivations, such as praise. We, as managers, must find ways to nurture autonomy so that work is significant for all because, in the end, companies are the combined work of everyone together.[73]

FOR SOCIETY TO WORK, WE HAVE TO TRUST

One definition of trust is being able to rely confidently on someone when you are vulnerable.[74] According to Ronald Burt and Marc Knez, trust is the "undertaking of a risky course of action on the confident expectation that all persons involved in the action will act competently and dutifully"[75] or "anticipated cooperation."[76]

Trust is an attribute of collective units that cooperate. Society can only exist when we trust each other. If there were no trust in the community, we would devolve into complete disorder and fear.

There is an inherent risk in trust, of course, and people can come to distrust other people and institutions. Distrust, fascinatingly like trust, also has a function because it quickly helps us discern a course of action.

According to David Lewis and Andrew Weight's sociological study of trust as a social reality, trust starts with familiarity. As we get to know the person or organization, we find evidence of trustworthiness. Getting to know people opens the door to confidence.

We also tend to trust when we know others who have already done so. Due to this psychological tendency, known as social proof, we assume that something is right if we know others already think that. If someone we trust trusts another person, we also tend to trust that person.

Trust contains an emotional component because having confidence involves making an emotional investment. When someone betrays our trust, we feel it emotionally. This factor is probably also why it is so hard to trust sometimes.

The final component of trust is behavioral. We act as if we knew how others will behave, even though this is not predictable. When we make that leap, the other person will tend to reciprocate[77] because reciprocity is a biological pattern rooted deeply within us. Scientists have observed in monkeys and dogs a tendency to return favors or disfavors. This imperative fosters cooperation and order in our societies.[78]

In the end, trust implies an expectation of positive outcomes. We are not sure the positive outcome will occur, which makes us vulnerable. Nevertheless, we trust because we believe the risk will be worthwhile.

THE BENEFITS OF TRUST

Studies show that when employees have a high level of trust in the organization, they are more satisfied with their work, perform better, and become better corporate citizens.[79] People who are trusted exert higher effort, often exceeding expectations. If they feel their supervisors entrust them with important tasks, they will do more and have more confidence in their abilities.[80]

Autonomy has been linked in other studies to goal setting, increased persistence and creativity, better performance, higher productivity with less burnout, and finally, an improved sense of well-being. Disclosure-based trust and the space for speaking freely and openly in the workplace promote employee motivation and engagement at work because it signals a psychologically safe space to interact.[81]

In a South African study that tested the nature of relationships between trust, autonomy satisfaction, and personal engagement at work, the authors, Marita Heyns and Sebastiaan Rothmann, found that employee engagement increased by 80 percent when managers supported their employees' autonomy. Full disclosure in management caused engagement to increase by 18 percent. Heyns and Rothmann write that when we place ourselves in others' hands, we accept being vulnerable, especially if we have no guarantees that the trust will not be violated when other opportunities arise. Trust, even per academic papers, is a leap of faith.[82]

One of Celaque's significant activities is to budget our buildings, which cost tens of millions of dollars. Adequately managing the budgeting process can make the difference between a successful project and a failure. Considering the size of each line item, when I was training a new team in our early days, it took some time for me to grow comfortable with our budgeting process because I had to learn to trust our team.

Now our team manages the entire process themselves: our Developments team sets their targets, finds savings, and makes decisions about where to spend more and where to hold back. Not only are they meeting their goals, but they are also innovating. They are improving our products with every iteration while keeping our costs below our limit. Finally, they are learning and growing as professionals.

When a company grows, it may add layers of middle managers who need approval from higher executives. Bureaucracy becomes inevitable, and the organization moves more slowly. Trust becomes essential to ensure that the company operates swiftly and profitably. As the work becomes more complex, following traditional, centralized decision-making takes too long to respond in today's demanding market. Furthermore, skilled workers operate best when they have as much autonomy as possible, reducing the company's vertical span and removing layers from the bureaucracy.[83]

Ideally, decision-making should be in the hands of skilled and great employees. Companies rely on employees' individuality and creativity in the knowledge economy and their ability to deal with complexity and autonomy. One way to promote employees' full potential is by creating work conditions that respond to how engaged they are with their jobs and the company.[84]

The same high level of decision-making, with no sacrifices in quality, can occur with fewer layers of middle management. The company will also be nimbler and better able to move quickly to meet market demands, and it can grow without succumbing as rapidly to the burden of bureaucracy.

Another benefit of having fewer layers is there will be less separation between everyone in the company. The feedback loops within the organization and with executives who set strategy will be faster. Communication is improved, and everybody understands the company's mission. Executives can alter course or develop the company strategy based on feedback from those in the frontlines.

I believe companies should stay as small as possible for as long as possible to offset the disadvantages of bureaucracy. And when you must grow, you can maintain a small company's flexibility by decentralizing and increasing autonomy, with the company's results in the hands of those doing the work.

With greater independence spread out to your teams, not everything will work out perfectly. Work may not be done as efficiently, but the rewards from building trust will be much higher.

We cannot be sure a trustee will honor that trust all the time. In one of his talks, Peter Kauffman, author of *Poor Charlie's Almanack: The Wit and Wisdom of Charles T. Munger*, says we have to risk the 2 percent of the times we'll be wrong to gain the 98 percent of the times when we will be right.[85]

Human nature motivates us to do everything in our power to stay safe. We will often miss out on the 98 percent because we are so consumed with protecting ourselves from the 2 percent.

As you trust more and more, you may find, as I did, that new and spontaneous projects start cropping up in different places to improve customer service and how your company operates. For the first residential building we developed when we founded Celaque, Astria, we hired Lily, a property management administrator who had a background in hotel management.

We had been recruiting for positions like this for a few years, but Lily showed us right away that we always should have been looking for someone with hotel experience for this role. She implemented all kinds of tiny tweaks that made a big difference to our residents.

For instance, she improved our maintenance response time. We work with many plumbers as part of our construction projects, but when a pipe in one of our finished buildings is leaking, they do not respond immediately. Lily found a new plumbing service provider specializing in other home maintenance solutions and could reply quickly.

She similarly developed a working relationship with the property manager of a neighboring building. They have been able to avoid misunderstandings between the two buildings and found ways to cooperate. Lily did all of this within her first six months at the company. We recognized the experience she brought to the job, and we gave her the freedom and authority to find creative solutions for the problems she faced.

Taking the risk to trust is worthwhile. You will find challenges, for sure, but most issues can easily be solved. Usually, each team takes care of their problems. They typically do not happen again because challenges train each person to be better in their work and teach the rest of the organization. As much as we would like to avoid mistakes, we must let them happen within set parameters and let the organization solve them as they arise.

DESIGN A TRUSTING ORGANIZATION

Teams need the information to make the best possible decisions, and it is in the company's interest to give employees all the data they need to do this. Providing more information, such as the company's business model and how each person contributes to the overall mission, communicates trust.[86] As managers, we might think we should guard confidential information to prevent leaks or conflicts. But the more access employees have, the more trust you build.[87]

We tend not to share some information, such as strategy or long-term plans, because we assume it is not relevant to everyday work. I have seen, however, how well people respond to being part of long-term plans as they develop. They naturally want to know where the company is going, and if they participate, they will do their part to achieve their overarching goals.

I frequently share updates on our long-term plans during our monthly, company-wide meetings, along with the obstacles we are encountering. As soon as we have important news for the company, such as obtaining financing for one of our future projects or a date for when we begin construction, we share it.

We recently began providing the top two or three metrics per department for the prior quarter to show how well we are doing, whether our construction project will be ready on time, or whether we are meeting our sales goals. Included are financial numbers about the state of our company that previously I would have kept confidential. These are essential to share internally because metrics provide clarity about the stakes of the work that we all do.

I also would have been hesitant in the past to share bad news, believing that morale could be affected, but we have started doing this. We had a few months where sales were not moving as we had projected. When I raised this in our company-wide meeting, I noticed some people were surprised and even concerned.

I explained the measures we were taking, but providing them with the information had an unforeseen consequence. It galvanized teams that are not usually involved in sales to take as many actions as possible to help our Sales team. Our Developments team, for example, prepared the building entrance faster than they had planned to, making the building as attractive as possible to buyers. We usually have more sales when the building is ready, and they helped get us there faster.

Everybody's work is linked to the result, making key metrics relevant for all. Once everyone has the needed information, the team can start planning and troubleshoot around any problematic hurdles.

It is essential to design your company in ways that show your employees you trust them. Overly bureaucratic organizations, centralized authority, not enough access to information and resources will communicate a lack of trust in the company's employees.[88] You can design the best structure, hire the best people, get the best software, and maintain the most important metrics. Still, if trust is not there to galvanize the whole operation, you will not realize your organization's full potential. Trust is both a pillar of Heptagram and a quality that permeates every interaction and helps hold the seven pillars together.

Heyns and Rothmann recommend creating an organization that maximizes trust and autonomy by encouraging an open work environment where everyone is free to question, speak, and act. Not only do we as leaders need to be careful and aware at a personal level of what we are doing that encourages and discourages trust, but we also need to design ways to ensure that communication is open.[89]

We can build spaces where employees can freely raise concerns and create a meaningful dialogue that includes dissenting opinions. During one of our company-wide meetings, we discussed a new building of affordable apartments in a central location for those in the middle class. One of our engineers said that if we wanted to make the final product more accessible, we had to lower maintenance costs.

I initially defended the current charge, and two others agreed. That is when I remembered to encourage discussion. I stopped myself, maybe a little too abruptly, and thanked our engineer loudly enough so that everyone in the company could hear. "That is a great point you bring up," I said. "We will examine how we can lower prices."

I asked him what had prompted that comment, and he said he lives in an apartment complex built by a competitor. The homeowner's association fees there are 40 percent lower than what we are charging. Had I not stopped to listen to him, I would never have considered lowering our prices.

Others in the meeting supported his point. We give out chocolates to the people who ask questions in our sessions, and he already had chocolate. To emphasize how significant his contribution was, I said, "Thank you for your suggestion," as I handed him another chocolate.

Not everyone speaks up in a company meeting as he did, so you can design other channels that allow open communication. Not only does that allow discussions of sensitive topics, but it signals that the company is willing to listen.

An example of this is creating opportunities for employees to make suggestions, comments, and concerns anonymously.[90] Another possibility is to ask open questions about existing problems and to use active listening techniques when the employees respond.

Finally, you can support autonomy by demonstrating how activities and tasks fit in with the outcome. Charlie Munger, investor, businessman, and vice chairman of Berkshire Hathaway, a multinational conglomerate, describes a psychological bias he calls the "Reason-Respecting Tendency." As cognitive beings, we enjoy using our intellect to solve mind games, such as puzzles and chess, for instance. We learn better when we know why we are doing something; if people combine their experience with "why," learning will be more profound.[91]

We built Celaque's operational structure to ensure efficiency and quality: we have designed procedures that address most of its operations. We have also tried to find a balance because too much can create excessive bureaucracy and communicate a lack of trust. We want employees to have guidelines for being certain nothing is left out, and they can then focus on what can never be scripted. If something is not working, the team is free to change it.

In many cases, leaders may unwittingly be the obstacle. When I managed Sales in Alianza, everything went through me, and I slowed the sales process. I checked all prospects and called them if something was not moving forward and the salesperson needed help. I negotiated every discount.

I quickly realized that our team would not be able to grow if I did not decentralize decision-making. I had to remove myself as the bottleneck so that our salespeople would be able to move faster. It took me some time to find out what I needed to do to give our team more autonomy. Our deals are not all standard. Each transaction is financially significant and customized. To facilitate how we approve negotiations and ensure we make the best decisions when making a sale, we set up a digital negotiation approval form.

On the questionnaire, we gathered all the questions we need to answer to cover all our bases. It has mandatory fields and a review process built in. Our sales representatives must fill in the transaction parameters, such as financing, pricing, and availability. Once they have completed the form, each salesperson submits it to a manager who can use it to make a decision quickly. Additionally, I implemented clear policies so that salespeople could now negotiate 85 percent of the deals.

Before we created the approval workflow, we had to go over every sale verbally one-on-one, and even so, we sometimes overlooked an essential factor. Now negotiations flow smoothly without having to remember all the steps for each transaction. Embedded in the questionnaire is the experience we have gleaned from past agreements.

Whenever there is something out of the ordinary and our salespeople need help, they escalate the problem. Our salespeople also communicate any issues that they confront, which they cannot solve. The rest, we manage via metrics. If we are reaching our targets every month, we know that we are on the right track.

Dependable Organizations

Ideally, we will make sure our organization is worthy of our employees' trust. People will trust their company if they see that it operates with integrity and is consistent in its actions. As employees get to know an organization, they observe how it reacts in different circumstances, and they especially learn how it responds to mistakes and achievements. They will also get an idea of how supportive the company is.

They will develop high trust from consistent and positive interactions with the company. A study conducted to examine the relationship between self-efficacy and workplace outcomes by Adnan Ozyilmaz, Berrin Erdogan, and Aysegul Karaeminogullari showed that when employees have a high level of trust in a company, they perform tasks well and the quality of organizational citizenship improves.[92]

Trust is like an account that increases with positive interactions going in every direction, creating a virtuous cycle. As the company, managers, and employees increase the level of trustworthiness, trust increases for all.

Participation in corporate social responsibility activities may help signal the organization's trustworthiness. Duane Hanse, Benjamin Dunford, Alan Boss, Wayne Boss, and Ingo Angermeier conducted a study that measured the relationship between corporate social responsibility and employee trust. According to their research, when employees know about a company's social responsibility initiatives, turnover decreases, and company citizenship behaviors increases. The study showed that corporate social responsibility is critical to employees and fosters confidence in the organization.

The study acknowledged the importance of investing in our communities but also pointed to the idea of letting those inside our companies, not just external parties, know about these initiatives. The study also encourages having employees involved in the planning of these activities and participating in them as a way of enhancing trust.[93]

For interpersonal trust to exist, there must first be institutional trust. Organizational confidence is crucial for companies. The more we develop trustworthy organizations, the more internal trust will evolve between people.

Personal trust tends to be based on emotions, whereas system trust is related to actions. Therefore, an organization is seen as trustworthy if it is operating as it should. As people get to know how a company behaves in different situations, they will trust it more. A company needs to have gained institutional trust to operate effectively.

Trust in the company serves as the framework for its interactions, causing it to develop in a virtuous cycle from institution to individual and vice versa, and between people. As it grows in one direction, it will grow in the next one.[94]

When the company operates in a geographic context where trust is not prevalent, creating a trustworthy organization is even more critical. A healthy organization can help to mitigate the lack of institutional confidence in the broader context.

Letting Go

Letting go is hard precisely because we want to avoid the pain that results from errors. Part of decentralizing is giving others the control we exert as leaders and managers.

I am not advocating putting your faith blindly in anyone. I have had the experience of dealing with human error that had significant repercussions and, in other cases, with people who did not honor my trust. One of our employees accidentally sent the wrong property deed to one of our clients to sign. This error meant that our client was virtually the owner of a different, larger property than the one he had purchased, and that could have potentially cost our company a great deal of money. Luckily, the buyer was a friend, and he helped us change the legal document. But this mistake made trust difficult. If the purchaser had been someone else, we could have lost the value of the property.

Another time, when we were buying a plot of land, the person responsible for the due diligence of the purchase did not see a contingency in one of the leasing contracts in the tens of thousands of dollars. We purchased the property, and only later did we realize the potential.

We had not taken it into account during the negotiation process and would have to take the loss if the contingency materialized. Luckily, we were able to solve the problem. Events like these stung, and they initially made me not want to trust again.

Nevertheless, I quickly realized that if the company was going to grow, I needed to let go. I had also learned valuable lessons from these mistakes, especially ways of fixing and preventing these problems. Some of it involved processes and policies; other solutions included placing the right people with the best skills for each of the roles. I also learned how to manage problems better once they occurred.

Gradually, you can try giving up control. As the founder of Celaque, I feel like the company is my baby. It has been hard for me to let go of something I am so attached to and protective of. Whenever I have a hard time giving up control, I make sure the worst-case scenario is not too risky and take the plunge.

If you are having a hard time trusting others, having the right guardrails in place can help, such as establishing a structure that can mitigate the effects of the problems that occur. Some areas of the company are just too risky and need to be supervised to ensure it is not exposed. Activities such as expense approvals and design decisions need procedures to check them. The right organizational structure and underlying processes and systems will ensure that you have minimized risks, and employees in these areas can have more autonomy.

We have review procedures in operations that need to be 100 percent accurate and have a high impact on our company. We have found that having more than one team member looking at the final product ensures that they find any errors. What one person does not see, the next person probably will.

For critical documents, the first person generates the report, the second performs a detailed review, and the third does a final overall check to ensure that everything makes sense. Having three separate points of view on critical documents guarantees that they will get different perspectives and be more accurate.

We apply this idea of levels of review to crucial documents that must contain no errors, such as our financial and tax statements and new client contracts and modifications to those agreements. Although our system's automation helps us generate the documents more quickly, we need to review them for mistakes or wrong information.

There are two benefits of the team collaborating to make sure they perform their processes with the highest quality. First, it ties the group closer together. We know we are all dependent on others, and we learn about each other's work, expanding the knowledge base within the company. If one person is continually reviewing another person's work, they each take on the same skills, and one can step in for the other during absences, such as vacation or maternity leave.

If you worry that the creation of autonomous teams will lead to a level of disorder, the concept of simple rules can help. Formulated by Donald Sull and Katherine Eisenhardt, simple rules are structures that channel undesirable behaviors or obstacles. To prevent a bottleneck, the team defines a simple guideline that solves the problem. The team then follows the procedure so they can avoid the issue in the future.

In Microsoft's software development process, bugs inevitably occurred. Typically, engineers solved them at the end of the project, but as soon as they fixed those bugs, new ones would crop up. The project timeline would be delayed. They decided to implement a simple rule. The overall number of bugs could not exceed the number of engineers times five. Therefore, they would stop the project to solve the bugs before moving forward. With this simple rule, the number of bugs is never more than can be handled. And now the products are delivered faster.[95]

PRACTICE MAKES PERFECT

Trust between people builds step by step. At first, the risk is small, and there is not much to lose. As we become more familiar with each other, we move to interactions with more risk because the results of our encounter can have a more significant impact. The more we continue to cooperate, the more likely we will trust in the future.[96]

When trust becomes a substantial part of the organization, it will become more entrenched in how work is done. At an individual level, the more you express trust, the more confidence you will receive. Again, it is a virtuous cycle. People will have faith in their manager if they receive it.[97]

Ultimately, trust is a decision to believe that relying on it outweighs the costs, making it worthwhile. I know because I have had to make that decision. I thought that if I let go and trusted, I would not be doing my job. As my company has grown and my role expanded, I have discovered that trusting is a significant part of my work. I must believe and let go, and then let go again.

The more I practice, the better I have gotten at it. I have also found trust liberating. The same number of problems, and possibly fewer, have arisen since I consciously decided to trust more.

THREE PROVEN TOOLS FOR TRUST-BASED MANAGEMENT

As you are setting up your company's organization with its accompanying business processes and information systems and measuring how well the company's actions align with its strategy through metrics, it will be necessary to simultaneously develop tools to communicate progress with your teams and manage operations. Some of the tools that I have found invaluable are company-wide meetings, management team meetings, and committee-based decision-making. These are all ways of fostering trust, one of the crucial elements of any successful organization.

Company-wide meetings will help you communicate the company's projects and initiatives as well as its metrics. Management team meetings will facilitate how you manage the company. They are also an excellent forum for analyzing company indicators and are useful for solving interdepartmental collaboration issues. Finally, committee-based decision-making is a mechanism that will help you harness the power of diverse groups to make the best possible choices for your company.

1. Company-Wide Meetings

Eric Schmidt and Jonathan Rosenberg's insightful book *How Google Works* introduced me to the value of company-wide meetings. According to the authors, the CEOs at Google held weekly Question and Answer sessions called "TGIF" meetings to discuss company policy and direction. The goal of the meetings was also to foster communication and transparency across the company.

At Google, the sessions were held every Friday afternoon, and everyone could ask questions. The questions could be related to any issue, including controversial topics, and the CEO's goal was to answer them as truthfully as possible.

As the company grew, they developed a system called Dory through which everybody could submit their weekly questions. The rest of the company voted the questions up or down, and the most important ones surfaced at the meeting. To ensure the responses addressed the issue, attendees raised green and red paddles depending on whether they felt the answer was accurate.

Different teams presented the projects they were developing in the meetings, along with images and mock-ups, so the audience could see everything before it was released. Many of the presentations given in these company-wide meetings contained confidential material that would be of interest to outside parties if it were leaked. The authors maintained that by trusting their employees with critical information, the company ensured that the information was honored and protected.[98]

I decided to try having meetings like this at Celaque. I was not 100 percent sure how it would work for us, so I tested a similar idea during one of our company's holiday events in December. A representative of each of the core teams spoke about their department's most significant achievements during the year. As people shared their experiences, I could see communication barriers breaking down.

People were hearing from each other about the main projects they had worked on, possibly for the first time. In some cases, they knew about the highlights; they were not familiar with the topics in other cases. It was like they had a new view into the inner working of each of the departments.

These presentations were short but very powerful. I wondered what else could be possible if we met consistently and everybody heard of new developments as they were occurring, instead of being presented only with the result. This concept from Google turned out to have an even more significant impact than I had initially imagined.

I was unsure whether the time required for the meetings could be justified because we had never tried anything like that in the past.

Still, I thought it was worth the experiment, and we started holding monthly, company-wide meetings.

Needless to say, we are much smaller than Google. Our product cycle times are long, so we decided to start with only one meeting a month. The timing has turned out to be exactly right for us.

The sessions have evolved with time, as we have experimented with a variety of topics and presentations. The overall goal is to provide a general survey of our company, goals, and key metrics. We also take advantage of these meetings to introduce issues related to our industry and technical aspects of our operations to learn more about the work each of us does.

During these gatherings, different teams present significant developments in the prior month and highlight where each unit is headed. Participants are encouraged to ask as many questions as possible and make suggestions for improvement as necessary. Each team selects the topics to ensure we present what matters the most within each of the company's functional areas. As CEO, I also provide a summary of the company's current challenges and general direction.

After the meeting, we have an informal session where we talk and spend time together. It is an excellent opportunity to meet new team members and build relationships across departments that operate in different physical locations. These encounters can greatly contribute to fostering trust among the participants and trust in the organization itself.

Even through the situation engendered by the COVID-19 virus, we continued to meet, albeit remotely. If anything, the meetings were more important then to bring the team together and to maintain our momentum. We realized that we needed to meet during the pandemic more often, so we met for what we called forums on the weeks we did not have company-wide meetings. In the forums, we gave any updates on what was happening. And, more importantly, three people from our team would talk about their experiences.

In one of our forums, they spoke about what they had learned as they transitioned to new roles. Then, after an invitation for others to speak, two other people spontaneously shared their experiences with the rest of the group. One talked about the difficulty of caring for a baby while both parents worked full-time jobs. Another spoke about how grateful she felt to be working in a company that never stopped operating. Through those shared spaces, I felt closer to our team than ever before.

Bring the Company Together

As in the meetings I described at Celaque, one of the benefits of company-wide meetings is that they physically bring the company together, especially if there are offices in different locations. Ideally, everybody should meet in the same place for these meetings because they can talk and get to know each other better.

Company-wide meetings can be a powerful tool to help develop a coherent culture within an organization. Each team can easily and naturally create its own identity because of the constant interaction between people. When every team comes together, people know they are part of the same company, and everyone can feel they are part of the same mission.

The more information you can share about the challenges the company is facing, the more everybody will feel ownership about what they are accomplishing; the meetings can give everyone a sense of belonging and contribution.

Share Innovation and Growth

Another advantage of these gatherings is that they promote the cross-pollination of ideas. As a company becomes larger, it becomes less likely that everybody will see each other daily. Different people in the team start seeing the issues the company is facing from varying perspectives.

Team members want to know how their work ties to the organization's overall strategy, and they are also interested in how well the company is moving toward achieving its goals. Company-wide meetings are a great place to present Key Performance Indicators. If everything is going well, they will be motivated by the company's success. If, on the other hand, there is no progress, a team that understands the organization's strategy and how each person is connected to it will be more likely to work toward ensuring the company achieves its goals.[99]

Present Major Projects and Information

In company-wide meetings, you can present significant initiatives as they are being developed. The benefit is that everybody knows about critical, ongoing projects; they are not only presented with *faits accomplis*. As each team's projects advance, the meetings also provide a deadline to ensure the different departments stay on track with their plans.

When each team presents, the team members develop more ownership over what they are doing. After someone has been working on a project for many months, hidden away behind a computer, unveiling the final product, and showing others the results can be gratifying.

Giving people ownership of ideas and products can significantly increase employees' engagement and satisfaction. Research shows that employees who have more psychological ownership of their work improve their happiness and satisfaction with their work. Furthermore, ownership is positively correlated with work performance and a sense of belonging to the organization.[100]

These meetings are necessary if you are regularly upgrading your systems, operations, and products. Before having these meetings, we did not have a formal vehicle for presenting and explaining these changes to the entire organization at the same time. Now we use the sessions to announce company-wide initiatives.

When we were revamping how we managed our processes, we presented the new framework, described the actions everyone had to take, and directed the team to general resources they would need. This discussion helped address and solve problems ahead of time and prepared everybody for what was coming next.

Company-wide meetings are also great moments for presenting information that impacts everyone, such as new hires for key positions. At Google, new hires are easily identifiable at the meetings by their different-colored propeller hats.[101]

Recently, at Celaque, we have started introducing one team member per meeting. We realized that even people who have been working together for a few years might not know important details about their colleagues and what they do outside of work. In each meeting, someone stands up and describes his education, what job he has done within the company, and his current responsibilities. Finally, the person shares anything meaningful about his personal life, including hobbies and volunteering work.

Everybody Learns

You can include a technical section where everybody learns at a basic level about what others are working on and how their work relates to the broader company context. By having a space where they can get introduced to the basic principles of a specialized area that is important to your company, everybody will do their work better.

A significant part of the work we do relates to building, and it requires specialized knowledge in construction. We often present different aspects related to how we build our buildings. During one of our meetings, the team learned why we do a soil survey and how to do it. A soil survey is essential before construction to determine what foundation a building needs. Unexpectedly, this presentation had a significant impact on everyone in attendance. Some people in operations had seen the reports but did not understand what they meant or their importance.

The format you use for company-wide meetings will be a continuous work in progress—they will evolve as your company changes. At Celaque, we keep experimenting with new topics and formats.

These forums can promote growth and innovation if you design them to communicate and share information transparently. They can provide a new space for people to learn about everything that makes you who you are as a company.

2. Management Team Meetings

As a company grows, its day-to-day operations become increasingly complex. Even when a company has the right structure in place, internal communication may not flow optimally. The interactions within the structure could be placing an undue burden on one person or a team within the company. A practice we recently developed is the creation of a management team to discuss ongoing issues. A management team can help your company facilitate more fluid and effective communication across departments.

I have been Celaque's CEO since we founded the company with just three people. The dynamics were different then—managing communications and the workload in a small team was reasonably straightforward. Now we are in the final phases of selling/leasing and managing three buildings, constructing another, and developing two other projects, with a few others in our pipeline. With many more transactions and interactions within the company, my role has shifted.

As we grew, I started to realize that I could no longer manage everything on my own. I could not be the problem-fixer for every challenge that arose, nor could I be the center for all communications. This transition came about slowly and took me by surprise. One of the signs that I found is that the workload and responsibilities had gradually increased to an unsustainable level.

Our management team meetings were meant to improve how we communicated and my role within the structure. This new initiative is one of the best implementations we have had at our company. The minute we had our first meeting, I felt an immense weight lifted off my shoulders. I had been responsible for the communication between teams, and I had not realized how heavy a burden it was for me until it was no longer my responsibility.

A management team frequently meets to discuss the company's direction and operations. The group discusses company-wide issues such as KPIs, personnel, budgets, and new strategies and initiatives in the meetings. The business meeting serves as a forum to communicate and collaborate across teams and to strengthen the ties between managers of different departments.

Additionally, it serves as a tool for accountability. In the meeting, each manager describes the work they are doing and presents each department's metrics. The rest of the management team can provide helpful feedback to improve weak metrics or places where there is room for growth.

The transparency of information across departments helps the management team make more informed decisions in the company's day-to-day operations. As a CEO, I am most often able to make better decisions simply because I have access to more information. The idea is to give others this same level of access to use it during their regular activities, and they can improve the quality of their work.

The meetings are also a great place to share team budgets and annual plans. Like metrics, budgets can be discussed by everybody on the team to ensure they are optimized. Every month, each manager presents her results. If a cost has gone over, the issue can be corrected promptly. The management team can provide feedback and share best practices across departments.

With no management team meeting, only the CEO has the perspective to set across-the-board targets. Management team meetings are useful in any area where the entire company must get on board and discuss an issue. If you have company-wide meetings, you can set the topics for that meeting in management team meetings.

The management team structure at Celaque has been a significant improvement in managing our company's information and decisions. It has made communication more fluid across teams, and it has empowered each of the departments even more as they manage their day-to-day operations and any challenges that arise.

3. Committee-Based Decision Making

Small, cross-functional teams can help you channel the same power of small groups evident in management team meetings. A cross-functional team is a group of people who act as a committee. Through these teams, you can also manage complex projects. They add a layer of accountability that can help companies make better choices.

When making a significant decision or guiding a project forward, different team members come together. Multifaceted areas or plans often require input from numerous points of view because there are many variables to consider. Tackling the topic using a variety of points of view will ensure that the best product will emerge.

Every company must make decisions in a complex environment. Company strategy, for instance, in any organization, occurs in the context of a market and economy. Boards of directors determine strategy and are an example of where different perspectives are useful to set the company's future path. You can also use these types of groups in other parts of the firm where decisions are essential or training the team in complex matters is vital.

Permanent cross-functional teams work better than temporary ones. The latter often have conflicts rooted in their functions and may lack clear accountability. They also rarely have enough time to solve differing perspectives. Permanent teams have been proven to work well in innovation groups, for instance. By bringing together different functional capabilities, they can launch new products or services.[102]

Select the Team

When you are putting together your cross-functional team, make sure you include every critical stakeholder. In smaller units, everybody who knows the topic can attend the meeting. In my experience, limiting the groups to six or seven people works best. A group that is too large can be unwieldy, and a smaller group will not benefit from the advantages of multiple perspectives.

You can try including team members with different strengths in the meeting so the group is well-balanced. A study that analyzed the results of venture capital investments tested the decisions of thousands of venture capitalists. It found that having diversity in the decision-making processes improved financial performance considerably, both for the company they were investing in and for the fund.

People tend to prefer coming together with others from similar backgrounds, a phenomenon known as homophily, but this preference does not translate to the business results we seek. A common ethnicity, for instance, decreased an investment's success by between 26.4 percent and 32.2 percent. The study found that at the time that the decision to invest was made, both groups had equally promising investment decisions. The difference in results came later as the teams helped form the company's strategy they were investing in and hiring and other important decisions in an early-stage company's growth. The creativity required by the investment teams was better delivered by those that were more diverse.[103]

Try to include as many different levels of experience, functional expertise, and backgrounds, including gender and age, as possible. We all see different parts of our context based on our education and practical knowledge. The more these various strengths can come together to achieve the same outcome, the better your product will be.

Meetings

An agenda is a great mechanism to make sure your session goes as planned. To ensure your cross-functional teams perform well, make sure someone is responsible for the overall group, the team has specific goals, resources, and deadlines, and that each of the members owns the cross-functional project's success.[104]

It is also useful to develop a set format to use in every meeting so that it always follows a similar flow. A regular rhythm will save time and help the discussion move along more smoothly. Distribute the agenda before the meeting and ensure it is precise and conscious of everybody's time.[105]

A program provides the structure for how you will spend the time and the discussion points. If there are no clear points, the meeting will likely veer off-topic, and you will waste valuable time. If you find you are often leaving the set topic for the meeting, it might help to have a "parking lot" for ideas you can discuss later.[106]

To guarantee that the project is moving forward, you can discuss the actions taken before the meeting and how the project is progressing overall. Manage only what needs to be discussed during the meeting. You can handle everything else beyond the session. For instance, updates that do not need to be considered further as a group can be sent in a message to all participants on the day prior so that you use no additional time.

Before ending the meeting, define the following actions, deadlines, and work assignments. Keep track of responsibilities and when they will be complete.[107] One helpful trick is to take notes that you want to follow up on in the next meeting on the current plan. In the following session, you can take those notes with you to make sure everything is moving forward.

I like to use these meetings as a tool for ensuring knowledge is passed on to others. I always aim to have people with more experience included in the meeting and newer team members.

Including new team members and other, more experienced professionals is useful not just in committee-type decision-making meetings but in any session. The more newer team members are exposed to the work dynamically, the better grasp they will have on how the process works. Of course, the entire group benefits from the fresh perspective of newer people who bring other points of view to the discussion.

During meetings, a lot can be discussed. If what happened during the meeting is not recorded, its impact will be lost. I recommend finding a way to document anything you have learned that will apply to the future to be institutionalized. The best thing you can do is find a way to absorb the best practices into the company's systems/processes/documents, so the know-how that you developed will stay in the company permanently for future reference.

There are many tools for managing and communicating effectively within your company in a way that builds trust. I have experimented with many and have found company-wide meetings, cross-functional teams, and management teams extremely valuable.

KEY TAKEAWAYS

- One of the challenges we face is infusing our companies with a sense of trust. When people are trusted, they are happier and more productive.
- One way to ensure that organizations are nimble is to push decision-making power to every part of the company. Decentralizing will also make your company more resilient and emergence-ready.
- Trust has many benefits. Autonomy has been linked in studies to goal setting, increased persistence and creativity, better performance, higher productivity with less burnout, and an improved sense of well-being.
- To design trusting organizations, it is important to openly share information and create opportunities for raising dissenting points of view.

- Another way to increase trust is by showing how activities and tasks fit into the larger scale of the company's objectives and results. As you are setting up your company's organization, you will find it necessary to simultaneously develop tools to communicate progress with your teams and manage operations in a way that makes all team members feel trusted and valued.

- Company-wide meetings are one tool that will help you communicate the company's projects and initiatives as well as its metrics. They are a way to bring the company together physically and develop a coherent culture of trust and transparency.

- Coming together to share ideas can foster innovation. In the meetings, you can present significant initiatives within the company so the entire team can become a part of them.

- Another useful mechanism for managing a company is creating a management team to discuss ongoing issues, its direction, and its operations. It is also helpful in establishing objectives and key results for the organization.

- A management team can facilitate more fluid and effective communication across departments.

- You can also create small, cross-functional teams to make decisions throughout the firm.

- When selecting your team, include every critical stakeholder and try to make it as diverse as possible.

- Trust is a virtuous cycle—people will trust when they have consistent positive interactions with the company. When trust becomes a substantial part of the organization, it will become more rooted in how work is done.

Six

Self-learning

In an economy where the only certainty is uncertainty, the one sure source of lasting competitive advantage is knowledge. When markets shift, technologies proliferate, competitors multiply, and products become obsolete almost overnight, successful companies are those that consistently create new knowledge, disseminate it widely throughout the organization, and quickly embody it in new technologies and products.

– Ikujiro Nonaka

Self-learning is the motor behind the growth of a company based on the Heptagram model. As elusive as it is crucial, it is the essence of a company's long-term success and resilience.

A large amount of information comes into a company each day. From interactions with suppliers to new regulations, we can learn from everything around us. Our teams also develop new knowledge every day. As each person within the company performs his daily work, he will learn, and this knowledge can be communicated and harnessed to amplify the entire company's knowledge base.

Ideally, the company can become an organizational learning machine that integrates all the beneficial information available within it to grow and evolve. When knowledge is institutionalized, everybody benefits.

TACIT VERSUS EXPLICIT KNOWLEDGE

Not all knowledge is the same. Japanese companies have long been aware of the distinction between tacit and explicit knowledge. Ikujiro Nonaka notes the difference in his book *The Knowledge-Creating Company.* "The centerpiece of the Japanese approach is the recognition that creating new knowledge is not simply a matter of 'processing' objective information. Instead, it depends on tapping the tacit and often highly subjective insights, intuitions, and hunches of individual employees and making those insights available for testing and use by the company as a whole."[108]

He goes on to describe how Japanese companies view themselves. "The more holistic approach to knowledge at many Japanese companies is also founded on another fundamental insight. A company is not a machine but a living organism. Much like an individual, it can have a collective sense of identity and fundamental purpose. This is the organizational equivalent of self-knowledge—a shared understanding of what the company stands for, where it is going, what kind of world it wants to live in, and, most important, how to make that world a reality."[109]

Tacit knowledge is the knowledge we develop as we start engaging with something new. For example, kneading bread is tacit expertise that one person can pass on to the next. It is knowledge that is personal and is hard to communicate. In a company, it is the practices, routines, and culture it develops.

Explicit knowledge is documented knowledge. It can be easily transmitted because it can be put into a system and formally communicated. Explicit knowledge would be the recipe for making the bread or diagrams that show how you manage workflows within a company.

According to Nonaka, a company can encourage a "spiral of knowledge" created by four types of knowledge transfers. One of the movements, tacit to tacit, occurs when one person teaches another her know-how. When a new person enters the company, she will learn the company ethos and its energy. She may not be able to communicate it, but she knows it when she sees it, and she can then teach it to other new members of the company.

Another example would be how a baker knows the dough she is making for her pie is just right and will turn out well. Transferring knowledge from tacit to tacit is not very impactful because the company cannot leverage it.

Then there is explicit to explicit, where documented knowledge is repurposed. An example at Celaque would be when we created a more usable form of financial statement. We aggregated the information for the entire company and were able to compare from period to period. This movement from explicit to explicit also does not amplify the company's amount of knowledge.

Where the spiral becomes powerful is in tacit to explicit and explicit to tacit knowledge transfers. A tacit to explicit knowledge transfer occurs when a person can translate his know-how into a formal document or instruction. Recently, our Developments manager made that leap with our development process. Through his work managing three of our developments, he has developed an extensive knowledge base. Before, he could train others in the know-how he had developed, but he did not have a formal mechanism to make that knowledge explicit.

Then, a few months ago, he took a tool we had developed, a sequential process we follow every time we develop a building, and amplified it with his know-how. He took each step and reinvented it with everything he had learned and continues to improve it. He will now be able to use this process and follow it for each new building we develop. It will make him, his team, and the company stronger.

Finally, as others take the new explicit knowledge that is available in the company and absorb it, they can widen their tacit knowledge base and start the spiral again. An example that occurred in Celaque is that we originally developed that same sequential process every time we closed a sale. When we saw how well it worked, we applied it to different company processes, such as our building process and the steps we take to hire a new person.[110]

This concept is one of the most impactful concepts I have learned. It resonated deeply with me because I realized that had been my main job at the company in the most recent years—making the tacit knowledge we develop explicit. Before learning from Nonaka, I understood the importance of widening the company's knowledge base, although I could not clearly explain what I was doing. Therefore, I could not teach others how to do it—move information from the tacit realm to being explicit and vice versa. Now, I can promote the virtuous cycle of knowledge.

Nonaka encourages our companies to embody the learning. And he is right; learning can become crystallized in objects and organizations. For instance, a car has programmed within it the knowledge of the engineers and designers who created it. When we use the car, we magically have access to the expertise these professionals endowed in the vehicle. While in the car, our capabilities are increased in ways we could not have done on our own.[111]

Likewise, knowledge can become embedded in an organization and make it bigger. It is not a simple undertaking, and what works for one company may differ from what works at another. Learning can cumulatively become part of your ethos. The more knowledge we aggregate into the culture, systems, and processes, the more wisdom will be available in the company as a resource for innovation and growth.

DOCUMENTING EXPLICIT KNOWLEDGE IN YOUR COMPANY

Information Systems

Knowledge strengthens a company's information systems. The more the technology integrates the organization's know-how, the stronger it will be. You can program your systems to embody the knowledge and experience already present in your company by having them follow the workflows that work best in your company.

This concept can involve simply making specific fields in the system mandatory, or it can be as complicated as programming workflows so that processes follow best practices. From there, you can proactively update the information systems with the most current knowledge.

We have been encoding knowledge into our systems from our company's beginning, and we continue to enrich them by using different methods. Our ERP software has been the primary tool we have used to enter our workflows. The software we use for managing our processes has also evolved and grown as we learn more and improve upon the work we do.

Once, we were in the middle of completing the financing for one of our projects. As part of the documentation, we had to list a group of apartments and their deed numbers. When we went to look for the information, we discovered our records were not complete. We did not have a central database for collecting a property's essential characteristics, such as location, size, legal information, and price. We had a spreadsheet with the apartments and their accompanying legal details, but much of the data was missing, and we could not rely on the information that was there.

We needed to compile the apartments' information rapidly, but we were slowed down by having to go back to the source to obtain all the necessary details and then add it to a document to send to the bank. This problem highlighted a deeper issue. We did not have a foolproof database with all the information needed for each of the properties we managed.

This experience prompted us to create a database in our ERP that is permanently locked and that nobody but a responsible party could modify. We then invested some time to upload all the necessary information about these properties into our system. We now store a list of all our inventory in our ERP. We save each property individually within the software, or the transactions related to the item, such as billing a lease, cannot be operated.

The form we use to store each property has all the required fields that must be collected, such as legal information and property characteristics. We even came up with some new parameters that we added as well, such as market price. Each item cannot be saved without all the documentation, guaranteeing that we consistently gather all the necessary information.

We set up these parameters using the knowledge that we, as a team, have learned over time. We then blocked modifications, except by one person. This way, we knew we could trust our information and had a readily available source in the future.

Processes

Ideally, you can program most workflows into company-wide systems, such as an ERP. Other procedures, such as the steps to close a sale, including physical resources or systems not linked to each other, can be documented in processes.

You can design the procedures to be simple and elegant. They should also integrate all the know-how available in the company. Still, processes need to be updated continuously, with each team member consistently verifying that his procedures are relevant and working as they should.

When you discover a mistake or a better way to perform a transaction, the knowledge learned can make its way to the company's modus operandi. Processes are an excellent channel to ensure that you include and update new knowledge about operations. If updating the company's procedures is simple, the team will be more inclined to make the changes. In the end, when a process is appropriately updated, you do not create more errors.

Manuals

It is vital to document policies as soon as you establish them. You can add to a document general protocols that you cannot program within systems or processes. These guidelines are overarching and should be part of the team's training.

Manuals can become the vehicle through which general departmental and company-wide guidelines can be implemented and updated. Without documented policies, it is challenging to implement change because the team will not have a single source of information. The more easily accessible the guidelines are, the more useful they can be.

It is better to have fewer documents because confusion can occur with too much information in different places. I recommend reviewing the material and updating it regularly because changes are inevitable, and from one period to the next, you may need to modify essential policies.

At Celaque, we encountered this problem as we undertook to systematize how we manage the buildings we develop. Although it is not our first time managing buildings, and we already have some systems in place, we are always upgrading how we do it. We are always adding new practices: from keeping a book for maintenance staff to report anything that happens during their shift to designing events so our residents can get to know each other such as movie nights and prizes for the best door decorations during Halloween.

How do we make all these new and useful ideas last? We are now managing two other buildings. Our goal is to absorb all the tacit knowledge we have learned in the past and apply it to future buildings through different types of documents.

As part of our building management organizational project, we have started to create processes and update our policies. We recently decided to combine all our building policies into one document, separate from the general department's policies. We can view them in one report instead of searching for information in multiple locations. We can also send the document to our clients, and we can replicate it when we start managing the next building.

Whenever we develop a new idea that later becomes a policy, we automatically know where to save it. This mechanism is valuable because we have many policies, including how to book events, how the pool works, and how to receive packages.

Keep Learning

None of these ideas work if the firm does not have a learning culture. One of the fundamental steps to begin to create this type of culture is to be able to, as a company, take in information. The company can learn to filter what is useful and what is not.

To do so, you can develop mechanisms for team members and others to communicate helpful ideas, which you and your teams can implement within the company. Suggestion boxes are traditional yet effective channels for communication. Issue logs can serve a similar purpose. So that they live on in the company, those practices then need to be communicated and standardized.

Creating a learning culture is also vital, and I believe the best way to create one is through example. If the company's leaders regularly emphasize corporate learning, you will communicate learning as a value. As learning becomes an ingrained value, everyone will participate in a learning culture that works together to improve how the company operates.

Another way to foster organizational learning is to build spaces for discussion and open conversation. They will help the team be more receptive to new knowledge, and team members will be motivated to make the company a learning machine. Company-wide meetings, management team meetings, and cross-functional teams can create these spaces and promote learning.

OUR COMPANY MANUAL: A STORY

Organizing a company's knowledge can be a real challenge. At my previous company, Alianza, our first attempt at documenting knowledge was to create an overarching company manual. We were a small company, and we thought one document would be enough. That manual taught me many lessons and has been the seed for the method we now use to document our information at Celaque.

A year after creating it, I looked at my former firm's 15-page manual and realized that nobody ever accessed it, including me. The manual contained pages of useful information, but even so, no one referred to it.

The company manual included:

- Company directory
- Company hours
- Policies by department
- Processes for, among others:

1. Receiving payments
2. Depositing cash
3. Paying expenses (how and how often)
4. Steps for making a sale
5. Marketing
6. Cleaning the office

Most of the information described processes, which we had defined as steps. People were trained on the basics when they started, but daily responsibilities took over, and they rarely accessed the document. It was easy to miss a step. Sometimes, the person training a new employee did not make the manual a part of the training because they did not use it and had forgotten about it. People mainly learned from tacit knowledge transfers.

I am the first to admit that I hardly consult manuals if they are not at my fingertips. We learned that merely gathering the information, turning tacit knowledge to explicit, was not enough. We needed adequate vehicles to make the information come alive for people as they went about their work.

Processes

I decided that we needed a live version of our daily work. I visualized written instructions that showed up as regular reminders with all the necessary information. All we needed was a platform and a way to set this up.

This need coincided with our implementation of processes and the software platform we used to manage them. We transferred a significant portion of the manual's information to procedures, which became steps for executing the work we needed to achieve. Each person was assigned a set of tasks, along with detailed descriptions and due dates. These showed up recurrently in each team member's to-do list, so they could not be ignored or lost.

Policies

We decided to compile our guidelines per department on our virtual server. This method seemed the best way to make this information available to our teams. Our policies include:

• Sales Policies:
1. Approved discounts

2. Managing client communications

- Property Management Policies:
  1. Guidelines for negotiations
  2. How to handle requests and complaints

- Marketing Policies:
  1. How our marketing cycles work

- Accounting Policies:
  1. How to manage invoice credits
  2. How to work with intercompany accounts

This arrangement has worked well for us.

INVESTING IN YOUR COMPANY

As you learn more about what works for your company, you will surely develop a project you want to implement or a new area of the business, which will institutionalize this new knowledge and drive improvement in your company.

Setting up an initiative for success does not happen automatically, but the investment of time does pay off. New projects or developments could range from an accounting process that gives you timely financial statements to the diversification of products into new markets. Whatever the case, the time put in to ensure a project will launch smoothly, similar to investing money with compound interest, will help you reach your end goal and increases its chances of working efficiently in the future.

Taking the time to envision how you want to implement the initiative will help you develop a more realistic plan. You may, for instance, want to implement set business processes for every area of your company for the first time. You may also wish to label them by department and area to give everybody a clear context of where they belong in the company's overall workflow.

Envisioning a global solution will help you develop a plan. Include in your plan measurable goals that include timing to make your destination clearer.

According to a study conducted by Edwin Locke of the University of Maryland, and Gary Latham, of the University of Toronto, individuals, groups, business units, and entire companies are more likely to reach their goals if they are specific and challenging to achieve. This study also found that being presented with close deadlines is more effective in making work move quickly than encouraging team members to do their best. And a goal can be either self-set, set by agreement, or assigned by a superior—all these modes will have the same effect to ensure a goal is achieved.[112]

Once your path is clear, the gaps between where you are and where you need to go will become more apparent, and you can plan the steps you need to take to reach your destination.

Designing and Setting up the Structure

The more detailed your plan, the more likely your project will be a success. As you are planning, include the design of the structure your project will operate from in the future. Try to add in steps that will make it sustainable and efficient in the long term. It is best to design the new area to be resilient from the start, with redundancies that will prevent the whole thing from falling apart should one part fail. This type of program might include hiring people, setting up processes, and investing in new systems.

Involve all stakeholders because together, you can create the best plan of action. Also, in my experience, I prefer to take more time in the design phase. It is easier to work out any potential problems during this phase because you can make changes on paper more quickly than when things are already in motion.

When we set up our accounting department for the first time, I used this type of anticipatory thinking to set up our workflows. Each time I added a new process, I would question the risks that could come. One potential issue was that one person could add the wrong value for a payment in the system, which might cause our financial statements to be off. Therefore, I decided to set up redundancies to reduce the possibility of errors. One of the ways we minimized this risk is by having more than one person review sensitive transactions.

As you go about setting up that new area of your company, think ahead to how you might save time and make it resilient so that it will last into the future.

Trial and Error

Allowing room for learning is crucial. The project rarely comes out perfectly on the first try. Iterate to come up with the best possible system.

Much of innovation is the result of trial and error. Often, the fear of failure stops us from exploring in the first place. But it is one of the most important avenues for learning. If we keep going and ideating, we can move past any disappointment faster, and the quicker we move through this cycle, the more the company will be able to grow.

Sometimes, a project we are engaging in has failed, but we have become so invested that it is hard to be objective. When a project has already failed, throwing more resources at it will not revive it. These are all sunk costs, as they are already spent and will never come back.

As soon as you determine that something is not working, I recommend quickly letting it go. Doing so will free up more space and resources to deal with other projects or reinvent the current one. It is useful at the beginning of a plan to have a set of expectations, and if you do not meet them by a specific time, you know that is when it is time to move on and reflect.

Once you have completed a project, whether successfully or not, take the time to review it with your team. Knowing what you did well is just as important as finding out what you can improve.

Once your postmortem yields its key takeaways, be sure they are institutionalized so they become part of the company's future. The more you practice letting go, learning, and moving on to the next project, the more adept you will become at implementing new projects. This process will, in turn, promote growth for your organization.

Updating

One of the constants of life is that nothing stays the same; projects and initiatives are subject to entropy. Processes and systems need to be updated regularly. Regulations, requirements, and team members all shift, and as a company evolves, we all learn and can always innovate.

Tweaking long-standing projects and standard procedures is more straightforward than starting anew. By looking for ways to improve what you have already implemented, you can help ensure that the time you invested produces the expected results. Here are some examples of the improvements our teams have made in their departments.

Construction

We need to train personnel to maintain our buildings once they are up and running. Instead of merely retraining construction workers on the job, one of our managers decided to create an apprentice program. He chose to take in promising candidates from our construction team and train them in the building's intricacies as it is being built. The idea is to teach them about each of the building's systems to know where everything is and the basics of how the electric and hydraulic systems work.

Sales

Our sales are few in volume and customized to each client. Our contracts need to reflect this reality, so we used Word documents in the past. They were quickly modifiable, and we could easily add the client's information and the property's characteristics in addition to any additional clauses. The problem was that they were not secure enough—someone could inadvertently delete a line, which would be hard to notice.

We tried different ways of solving the problem, like programing the possible clauses into our ERP software and then producing the document from the system. Yet, nothing could compete with the simplicity and speed of our Word documents. I could not let it go because I did not think our Word documents would work for us in the long run. Finally, a year after we started experimenting, inspiration hit me.

We decided to create PDF templates in which 95 percent of our clauses are unmodifiable, and from there, we could fill in a few fields. Additionally, we assembled a document that we produce from our ERP with the transaction's values and all our special clauses. Not only are our contracts more secure, but we can create them in half the time they took before.

Accounting

In this structured discipline, we do not often think of the role that creativity can have. Of course, the accounting rules always need to be strictly followed, but how we get our work done is up to us. For instance, we could not reconcile our accounts with one of our suppliers after one of our projects. The amount that we had as a payable to them did not match the receivable they had on their books.

Throughout the construction of that building, we thought we agreed each time we paid a check. But in the end, we had a substantial financial difference that took us weeks to sort. We knew we needed a new solution.

Instead of letting our accounts reconciliation pile up during our other projects, our accounting team decided to sign a document after each invoice payment that acknowledged that the statement was fully reconciled. We had never done this before. The solution was a creative fix that ensured we would not have the same problems in the future. Our accounts are up to date in our next project, and although this may seem like a simple improvement, it will save both our supplier and our company many hours of work.

This experience showed us that we could put in the work whenever we located a problem and find a solution. At the beginning of a company's life cycle, you will be rushing to set up different areas, such as accounting and marketing. Once your company is functional and operating well, the work has not ended—you will always find areas of the company that need to be updated or improved. I heard an entrepreneur and CEO say once that he was continually questioning each part of the product cycle, starting with research and development, moving into manufacturing, marketing, and operations. Once he finished going through the cycle, he would begin again. Your path may vary, but the concept will help the company continue to improve.

Even more importantly, we can create organizations that are learning, living systems. By teaching others the "spiral of knowledge," we can harness our human ability to learn. The aggregate knowledge base will help our companies evolve to fulfill the visions we have for the organizations we have created and built.

KEY TAKEAWAYS

- Tacit knowledge is the knowledge we develop as we start engaging with something new: its routines, practices, and culture. Explicit knowledge is documented knowledge that can be formally communicated.

- A company can promote knowledge transfers between one type of knowledge and the next. The most impactful transfers occur between tacit and explicit and vice versa.

- A tacit to explicit knowledge transfer occurs when a person can translate his know-how into a formal document or instruction.

- You can document explicit knowledge in information systems, processes, and manuals.

- When you are starting something new, leave room for experimentation. Once your initiative is up and running, keep updating it so that it always stays current.

Seven

Plasticity

As our world continues to change rapidly and become more complex, systems thinking will help us manage, adapt, and see the wide range of choices we have before us. It is a way of thinking that gives us the freedom to identify root causes of problems and see new opportunities.

— Donella Meadows

Heptagram is far from a closed system. It is a method to design companies that can adapt swiftly and efficiently to rapidly shifting environments. Plasticity is one of its fundamental pillars. The Coronavirus crisis has shown us that forces unknown can emerge and alter our plans at any time. Without plasticity, we are rigid and slow to adapt. When you design your company structure and processes with plasticity in mind, neither external nor internal changes can shake your foundations. Plasticity is strength without rigidity, and it is a concept that is deeply rooted in business management theory.

Frederick Taylor was one of the first business management consultants. He was an industrial-era management thinker who worked to bring the production processes in factories to maximum efficiency. Taylor assigned highly specialized tasks to individual employees and figured out how to shave off significant amounts of time from the overall production. He believed that, by applying systems thinking consistently to the workplace, he could discover ways to increase productivity and employee satisfaction.[113]

Taylor was accepted to Harvard University, but he decided instead to become an apprentice at Enterprise Hydraulic Works due to his poor eyesight. He then became a supervisor at Midvale Steel Company and a general manager at Manufacturing Investment Company, a paper products company. Taylor was able to focus on increasing productivity at both organizations.

When he noticed he could not motivate employees to be more productive, he turned to their managers for help. He decided that managers did not have enough information to oversee their teams properly. Managers needed more technical knowledge about how to operate machines, for example, as well as psychological data such as how to manage worker fatigue. To give them more information, Taylor began analyzing how to make production processes more efficient.

Once he had taught the managers, they became responsible for finding more efficient production methods and training employees. Work had to be carefully measured to provide feedback. In 1893, Taylor left to become a consultant, and some of his clients included Engine Building Company and Bethlehem Steel Company in Pennsylvania.[114]

Taylor applied scientific principles to his observations about the production process, and in 1911, he published *The Principles of Scientific Management*.[115] The word scientific in the title spoke to his attempts to find widely applicable principles to increase productivity everywhere. Taylor wanted to create a science that would be capable of analyzing work. He believed the tasks performed in factories had enough merit to be studied just as medicine was.[116]

In his book, he described scientific management as, "Science, not rule of thumb. Harmony, not discord. Cooperation, not individualism. Maximum output, in place of restricted output. The development of each man to his greatest efficiency and prosperity."[117] Taylor's work is based on three principles: the functional separation of labor, the breaking down of work into its fundamental pieces, and the removal of teamwork.[118] His ideas helped shape current management theory.

Taylor's commitment to scientific principles led to the creation of management as a profession. His work was not without controversy, enough that even during his lifetime, unions rejected his theories.[119] Taylor is sometimes blamed for dehumanizing work and making it less meaningful by analyzing it in smaller parts. He was seen by some as being against workers and not caring about the demand for the work they performed.[120]

Nevertheless, his impact on management theory is irrefutable. Some of the areas he later influenced include industrial efficiency, organizational behavior, measurement of work, standardization, identification of individual tasks, and how they are managed.[121]

As managers, we are descendants of Taylor's conceptual framework. We value productivity and efficiency and doing the most with the resources we have. His ideas regarding the minute analysis of the manufacturing process gave rise to our constant examination and evaluation of a company's business procedures to ensure productivity. Taylor's influence is apparent today from the detailed production methods and how executives manage entire corporations.[122]

Taylor was alive during a time that was vastly different from the one we inhabit today. The speed of communication and the interconnectedness of our world today means we can do more, but this also makes us more interdependent and, therefore, part of a complex web.

World economic markets can be erratic, supply chains are vulnerable to failures because of unforeseen events, and natural disasters are unpredictable. Emerging threats such as climate change, which over time have increased the impact of natural disasters, urbanization, and pandemics, can accentuate already existing risks.[123] [124]

DISTINGUISHING OUR ENVIRONMENT

It is our interconnectedness that leads to the complexity we inhabit. Complexity in systems and contexts has been amply studied. Complexity theory observes systems that are "complex, deterministic, non-linear, and dynamic."[125]

David Snowden and Mary Boone developed one method, the Cynefin framework, to help leaders understand our environment. This framework gives us new points of view and helps us solve the problems we are facing. It shows that we, as leaders, face five contexts: simple, complicated, complex, chaos, and disorder. Disorder occurs when we are unclear which of the other settings predominates.

Once we distinguish between these contexts, we can choose the right tools and management style for each situation. Complexity is more predominant than we would believe, and it requires responses that might seem counterintuitive, making it especially useful to know which setting we are in.

Simple

Cause-and-effect relationships dominate simple contexts. These relationships are clear to everyone. Processes, supervision, and management work well here. An example is an accounts receivable payment process, where the outstanding balance is known to all. Once the payment is received, a confirmation is sent to the customer. If the payment is late, policies describe late fees or other charges. The work is clear-cut, and little discussion is needed.

Problems can arise in simple contexts, however. If a leader reviews only condensed information, he may not notice when the context is transitioning to complexity. Also, if things have always been done a certain way, the possibility of fresh perspectives may be missed. Finally, leaders can be complacent about a simple process when no problems have occurred in the past, and they can easily overlook a crisis. Complacency is one of the main reasons for failure in the simple domain.

Leaders can encourage autonomy and keep communications open to avoid these potential problems so that they do not miss critical changes. If possible, they can create communication channels for people with divergent views to voice their ideas.[126]

Ray Dalio describes a way to ensure these views come to light using an issue log. In his company, Bridgewater, he implemented an error log that would make sure problems were communicated so that the people involved could find their root cause. If something did not go well, the person who found the issue had to record it in the log along with its severity and the person responsible for it. This practice means the problems are brought to managers instead of being the manager's responsibility to seek them out.[127]

Dalio proposes creating metrics around the issue log, so the quantity and types of problems can be measured. This log led to solutions to the issues and the implementation of improvements at Bridgewater, but the issue log helped change behaviors in the company. Instead of people feeling bad when someone pointed out a mistake, people saw the benefit of finding errors and fixing them.[128]

I was fascinated with the issue log as a tool to see the problems in designing a company's structures and workflows. Dalio also credits it with changing company culture. It helps people see mistakes as a regular occurrence and helps to bring errors to the surface.

When I implemented this at Celaque, I made it as simple as possible—it is just a spreadsheet that we share across the company. Anybody can modify it. We have columns for the date, the issue, who is recording it, what team is responsible, whether the case is closed, and the resolution.

It took some time for people to understand how to use the tool thoroughly. For example, they would not log every problem as it occurred or did not update it once a case was closed. Sometimes, they did not explain the problem clearly.

Then, when people started entering more information, I began to see its benefits. I noticed issues that bridged several departments. Many of these issues were hard to solve if you could only see the problem from one team's perspective.

Sometimes the same question was entered on more than one occasion, but both entries looked like different issues because they were addressed from different angles. When the problem appeared more than once, especially if different people had logged it, I took it as a sign that the problem was entrenched or that it had had a significant impact. Starting with the most important ones, I took the lead in solving all the original issues. I had heard some of the errors before, but once they were on the log, explicitly laid out, their root causes were easier to find.

The most common issues were related to communication between departments, where one team was not informing the other with enough detail or on a timely basis. For instance, we discovered that one of our departments was not letting our Projects team know all the details they needed to have our office spaces ready for customers on time. One mistake had already occurred when an unneeded wall was built in an office.

A year before the Developments team logged the problem, we had designed a report to communicate from the first team to the next group the type of work they needed to do to prepare the office spaces. We had never used the log before, and the Properties team had not remembered to implement it and instead developed a parallel, spreadsheet-based report.

The spreadsheet was functional, but mistakes were occurring because it lacked information. We all agreed that the original report would work much better. We then had a training meeting where everybody settled on how to use this document and even improved it. We have not had another problem in that space again.

Every time I open the issue log, I am impressed with how useful such a simple tool can help a company run smoothly.

Complicated

A complicated environment may be challenging to manage, but it responds to cause and effect. There may be more than one answer, even if none of the solutions is easy and require expertise. Not everybody can discern how to solve problems in this context. Solutions call on research into the many different options and in determining which one suits the situation best.[129]

Designing a building is a complicated endeavor, involving a team that includes architects, engineers, property managers, and finance experts. All this collaboration requires specialized knowledge and training, but with the proper education and experience, the causes and effects are discernible, and we can complete a building's design.

In a complicated environment, experts may rely on patterns that have always been used in the past, ignoring fresh perspectives from non-experts. Competing experts may also reach impasses where they cannot agree. Decisions in this context may not be fast because we need to consider many inputs.

Complex

A complicated setting resides in the world of "known unknowns," a complex environment deals with "unknown unknowns." A complex situation is affected by many different factors, and no right answer exists. According to Snowden and Boone, most companies' decisions and events are complex because any individual element can lead to unpredictable effects. Experimenting can cause patterns to emerge, and only when we view a situation in retrospect can it be understood.

The housing market lies in a complex scenario because it so often depends on the actions of individuals. They respond to each other and the activities of one move with the next actor's actions, making it extremely difficult to predict the next shift.

One of the biggest temptations in a complex context is to impose a controlling and overly hierarchical organization, which can easily backfire. This approach is the opposite of the more experimental ones that complexity requires. Also, when you experiment, a higher tolerance for failure will be helpful because failing is essential. Too much control will cause you to trip up on yourself. Instead, leaders can set up the environment, allow behaviors to emerge, and find ones favorable for the company.[130]

Responding to complexity does not involve throwing out efficiency. Our work compels us to create strategies that aim to improve proficiency in the parts that reside in the simple and complicated contexts and develop approaches whose goal is to respond to complexity. Processes, systems, and lines of responsibility help solve issues in the first two paradigms.

We need different tools to approach complexity. Some include sharing information across the board and empowering the teams.

Autonomous teams work well, as does decentralized decision-making. Other mechanisms are experimentation and allowing the emergence of patterns and behaviors without trying to control them.

Chaos

A chaotic context contains no cause-and-effect relationships and is simply noise. Chaos exists in emergencies. No patterns will likely arise, and instead, you must deal with the immediate consequences of the situation. As you impose some stability on the circumstances, you can move them into complexity and work from there. Managers should keep in mind that chaos can be an excellent opportunity to introduce innovation. As you are dealing with the emergency and seeing what caused it, you can find ways to make improvements for the future.[131]

The COVID-19 virus created a situation that, at times, pulled us into chaos. It was often unclear what actions we needed to take, and all we could do as a company was to stabilize our organization. It was also a great time of opportunity. Opportunities for new products and services materialized out of nowhere.

Moreover, previously hidden problems within the company's structure, teams, and processes became evident in a way they had never been. I listened to see what we could improve for the future from day one and was able to make changes that, in the past, would have been much more difficult.

As leaders, we must recognize that the world around us is continuously changing. Its evolution has many advantages, such as information's ability to travel anywhere, but there are also numerous challenges, including vulnerability. Our world has become more complex. What may work in one context may not work in a different one. It is crucial to understand what setting we are in to better deploy the tools we have available to succeed in today's world.

We know how to deal with simple and complicated contexts, which require order and methods. Processes and systems are essential for dealing with known paradigms that require expertise. These can efficiently help us effectively reach our desired goals with minimum effort.

We are rarely prepared for complexity and chaos. Complexity requires other tools. If we try to approach it using control and management techniques, we may have unwanted effects. First, we need to recognize what context we are dealing with. With that knowledge, we can devise ways to respond to the world around us proactively.[132]

MAKING SENSE OF THE COMPLEXITY AROUND US

An organization is not a rigid set of processes, systems, and people who execute its operations. Donella Meadows, in her book *Thinking in Systems: A Primer,* says that companies are systems. She defines a system as "an interconnected set of elements that is coherently organized in a way that achieves something." Organizations are systems, and so are human bodies, ecosystems, and schools.

A football team can be a system. Its elements include the coach, the players, the fields, and the ball. Its interconnections are the strategy, how players communicate, how physics controls the movements of players and the balls and the rules of the game. The team's purpose can vary. It can be to win games, make money, have fun, or all these together.

A system is not a set of elements to be controlled. It can, says Meadows, "exhibit adaptive, dynamic, goal-seeking, self-preserving, and sometimes evolutionary behavior."[133] It is essential first to understand it as a whole: its elements, how they are connected, and what a function is.

Sometimes we do not know a company's underlying goal because its behavior drives outcomes that differ from its stated purpose. In business, the most common goal is to increase profits. However, the objective of the system may be to grow and to continue doing so.[134]

A company does not operate in a vacuum; it resides in a context that can be complex. With a deeper understanding of the current system and the context in which it operates, we can use our knowledge of how systems work to move it in the direction we want and away from behaviors that are not conducive to the results we seek.

Defining Resilience

According to the Oxford English Dictionary, resilience is: "The capacity to recover quickly from difficulties; toughness. The ability of a substance or object to spring back into shape; elasticity."[135] Another definition is: "The capacity of a system to absorb disturbance, undergo change, and still retain essentially the same function, structure, and feedbacks—the same identity."[136]

A resilient organization is flexible and can adapt to circumstances and change as the context shifts. It can recover from failures quickly and adjust itself to respond better to what is happening around it. According to Meadows, resilience measures how well a system can prevail in a changing context. It is not frail, nor fixed and unyielding.[137]

Resilience is a vital characteristic of a system, and we can promote resilience, or we can undermine it.

If a key employee takes an unexpected leave of absence, a resilient organization will reorganize and maintain a similar level of efficiency. This adaptability is possible because perhaps other employees were trained in the same area, the processes in that department are well-documented, and the company's software fully supports the entire team. If a new employee eventually has to be hired, the organization can quickly get the new hire trained.

A resilient company is strong. The networks and underlying information systems and processes are robust yet flexible enough that they all can weather change. They do not depend on any given person but are instead institutionalized. The organization's knowledge is embedded in the way it operates.

This future contingency is also why founders and CEOs should prepare a succession plan as soon as they take the reins in any organization. One can never know how things will change, so the company should be able to stand on its own.

Resilient systems are not static. Breakdowns may be part of the system it acts upon, and a resilient organization will be able to re-establish itself and recover. On the other hand, organizations that are unchangeable over time can lack resilience. To maintain stasis or to increase productivity, systems may sacrifice resilience.[138]

A company's structure can encourage employees to become highly specialized because that increases productivity. In this type of organization, each person only knows how to do one part of the whole and nothing more and cannot see the full view. Like Frederick Taylor's factories, this structure may produce the results the company expects, using the least amount of time and resources possible. But that does not promote plasticity.

Companies become less resilient as they grow and become more stable and mature. They become more susceptible to shocks and can take longer to recover. This lack of resilience stems from a bureaucracy that tends to accompany growth.

These companies may favor obsolete practices and systems and become blinded to changes in their environment. They are less able to distinguish threats until it is too late, and the problems have already become a crisis. The organizations that can embrace change and shift with it can better respond to this changing world.[139]

At Celaque, I have focused on plasticity, making our company's functions as resilient as possible. When we were a smaller company, we had few people and depended a lot on each person. I feared people leaving because I felt we were vulnerable if people with critical knowledge were no longer at the company. This feeling prompted me to design the company better.

One of the ways we have experimented with resilience is redundancy. We now make sure that a few people know how to perform all the team's workflows within each of our teams. As the company has grown, it has become easier to have more than one person with the requisite knowledge in each group. We have also designed all the relevant support documents to be self-explanatory. We can easily reassign and move our processes when there are changes.

Celaque's ability to withstand changes without losing its capacity to operate consistently continues to be one of my priorities. The unprecedented situation we faced as a result of the COVD-19 pandemic tested everything we had designed and built at Celaque from its inception: its organizational structure, its systems, its processes, and its ability to deal with complexity. Its resilience, especially, was put on trial.

I was most grateful about all that time we had spent implementing cloud-based systems, which allowed us to transition smoothly to remote work, with no downtime, from day one. Because we were used to working through our software, it was a matter of continuing our work from a different location. Then we moved all our physical meetings to digital platforms. Our monthly, company-wide meeting and all of our department and cross-functional meetings moved, as scheduled, to Zoom.

The work of some of the people in our Developments team was significantly disrupted because it was presence-based. Our Sales team also saw their work dwindle because, as the shock of the situation sunk in, followed by the economic aftermath, our sales floundered. These two teams moved more seamlessly to support our other departments, Properties, Corporate, and the rest of Developments, which were either on the frontlines or had a backlog of projects.

Our goal was to get to the other side of the situation stronger and more resilient. That period was a great time to listen and improve our operations. It made very apparent some of the company's areas that had not kept up with the rest. For instance, although we were receiving most of our customer's payments digitally, our payments to suppliers were still completely manual. The virus helped us see the necessity to move all our expenditures online, saving our suppliers and us much time and effort in the long run.

Increasing Resilience

When you optimize a company's maximum efficiency by doing exclusively what it does well, you will receive short-term gains. However, the company will become less resilient as it becomes vulnerable to changes and shocks. On the other hand, if it does many different things or one thing in many ways, it is more resilient but less efficient. By increasing redundancies and not designing the company to obtain the maximum return, you incur costs that make the company less profitable, at least initially, but more resilient. Managing for plasticity, therefore, comes down to finding the balance between short-term profits and long-term resilience.

One way to increase a company's resilience is by introducing diversity—of people and organizational procedures and types of functions and responses available. If the system experiences a shock, a crisis that it needs to manage, a resilient company can respond in various ways. Diversity will allow flexibility and create different options.

Another way to promote plasticity and foster resilience is by empowering autonomous management within the company's various groups. If decision-making is subject to centralized governance, that sort of feedback on time-sensitive information may take too long to produce a timely response, leading to problems within the company. The more decentralized the organization becomes, the more resilient it is.

Organizations that excel at plasticity are also modular. Too much connection between departments or teams reduces plasticity because shocks travel more quickly from one unit to the next. Strong internal links and freer interunit links increase resilience. When a problem arises in one group, these loose linkages will allow other teams to organize themselves better and respond to the situation.

Plasticity encourages innovation by allowing grass-roots initiatives and room for experimentation. A resilient organization works to create more space and ultimately embraces change and turbulence. It does not constrain or ignore it.[140]

Introducing plasticity into an organization is a bottom-up exercise, as well as a company-wide effort. These initiatives can include the fostering of diversity, interconnectedness, company continuity, and feedback from outsiders.[141] From an organizational perspective, it is essential to develop a more robust culture and leadership.

Other ways a company can boost plasticity are:

- Supply chain management: promote alternate channels for sourcing, supplier innovation, visibility of product locations and arrival dates
- Human Resources: advocate learning, new and different points of view, and a healthy organizational culture
- Customer service: find ways to offer customized services, identify and respond to market shifts
- Product and service development: create different product configurations, encourage innovation, reduce the time it takes for a product or service to go from new idea to deployment.[142]

Freedom

Teams within companies and companies themselves solve their problems by finding ways to self-organize. Self-organization is a system's ability to take its current structure and make it more sophisticated and evolve. An example would be how communities have taken different elements available in society, such as bricks, cement, glass, and the need for more space, and created skyscrapers. It is a natural characteristic inherent in systems. It is pervasive, and it can be hard to eliminate.

Instead of trying to control everything, we can encourage self-organization, which does not necessarily unfold in a clean and organized manner. Self-organization can develop new structures and workflows. Because it requires experimentation, it may make us uncomfortable,[143] but the rewards can be immense.

By setting up an organization, we as leaders, founders, and CEOs seek to harness the ability, intellect, and power of a group of people to create something more than the sum of its parts. Often, in the name of productivity, stability, and order, we seek to control the way things operate and, in so doing, drown out initiative. I know; I have done it myself. This behavior is short-sighted and a disservice to the building of an organization. In the end, it is futile because self-organization in systems is pervasive, and thankfully so.

Letting the company solve its problems and organize how it works to achieve its purposes is a big part of allowing your company and its teams to reach their full potential.

Listening, Paying Attention, and Mapping

Sometimes it is best to take no action and listen to what is happening. Listening can provide useful information about what is occurring and help us act, when we are ready, in the best way possible.

As you discover what others around you are saying, listen to views instead of your own beliefs. One of our main cognitive biases is confirmation—a search for evidence to support our thoughts and beliefs.[144] We tend to filter out what does not match our views, but listening to these opposing opinions can broaden our minds and our way of thinking.

As you listen, you can analyze how and why a system is behaving as it is. Networks have inherent behaviors that can be positive or undesirable. A behavior is how a system or company is performing over time, and this can include many results such as evolution, growth, decline, or stagnation. To determine a company's behavior, you can use a systems-based approach that involves analyzing historical data. Practices that persist over time can reveal the structure that supports the system, and that will provide the information needed to examine how comportment occurs and why.[145]

You can then diagram the system's organization and discover its inherent characteristics. Once you understand the company's structure causing the behaviors you want to change, you can rearrange the structure and the conditions that underlie it. During this reorganization, you can decrease the likelihood of negative actions occurring and create incentives for the behavior you seek.[146] But you can do this only if you first listen to what is happening around you and understand the conduct in the system.

Listening and analyzing will help you truly understand how your company is currently working so you can help free any constraints that are stopping the company from reaching its full capacity.

One of the behaviors I was curious about in our company was why, after we defined ourselves as a functional organization, our teams were not fully autonomous. I noticed that some problems did not get resolved until they reached me.

Although I had a few theories, I was not sure why this was occurring. I started listening. I compared teams that were more autonomous with others that were less independent. One thing I considered was that I was the only person who saw these problems. The company operated well, but I needed to empower our teams more so we would be more agile.

That is when I implemented our management team meetings. There, each of our managers presented the issues they were facing. They also presented their projects. I sat back and let them take control. Little by little, everybody saw how they were connected, and they started understanding each team's role within the larger company. This intervention, along with others, such as company-wide meetings and the use of metrics, has empowered them.

I also learned through listening that although our managers were making do with the personnel they had, we needed to hire more people. Our operation had quickly grown, and we needed to expand our size if we wanted our innovations to keep pace with our growth.

Safe-To-Fail Experiments

If we view our companies as systems, we may find they are composed of independent parts that work with each other in ways that are neither obvious nor easy to grasp. Some of a system's behaviors may lead to negative results that you want to change.

Testing can provide useful information about what is happening around you. Sometimes curiosity and awareness of how a complex environment works produce faster results than rigid plans and indicators. Safe-to-fail experiments are controlled, scientific tests that will allow you to probe your circumstances so you can learn more about your context.

To plan a safe-to-fail experiment, you start with a hypothesis and then test it in a fast and uncomplicated way that can also be fun. In the final phase, you learn from what happens.[147]

These experiments help you expand your point of view. A safe-to-fail test aims to change how the system behaves, not to obtain a specific result. A safe-to-fail experiment will be small and not involve the entire company, which would be challenging to orchestrate. Trials such as changing the way furniture is laid out in an office to encourage communication or buying a cake to mark a special occasion, on the other hand, are straightforward and doable.[148]

The experiments start small but can be scaled upwards if they go well. You can easily cancel them if they are not going well. A safe-to-fail experiment will probably fail, and when it does, it should be easy to fix.[149] Failing must be okay. If the company will end up in trouble or someone's safety is in peril, then the experiment is not safe.[150]

The goal is to learn from these experiments. The data collection does not have to be sophisticated, just parameters and stories about how things are shifting in a different direction. If you are interested in increasing communication, you can design experiments to learn how to encourage it. As you experiment, data about how people are talking more to each other can at first be qualitative, while you can gather more quantitative information. Be aware of our tendency toward confirmation bias.[151] Data that disproves our assumptions is often the most valuable and where we can make more impactful changes.

If you have a hypothesis about a new product idea, you can start by introducing a one-time trial with long-time clients to see whether they like it. That will give you information for deciding whether to continue the process.

We wanted to see if the people who lived in one of our buildings wanted to know each other better and what it would be like when everybody came together and started talking.

We decided to invite everyone to an afternoon event called "Semitas and Coffee." Semitas are a local pastry—a toasted, sweet bread with sugar on its top and edges. The event followed its own rhythm, and we planned nothing beyond the food and the place. As our team took over the coffee machine, people talked to each other, sometimes for the first time. They gave us valuable feedback about the management of the building and generally had a good time.

"Semitas and Coffee" was a success, and we made it a regular event. Now, different team members join the activities that we plan, and they have reported that people enjoy meeting each other and our team. They are pleased to be part of a community. I am happy that the event went well, but as a safe-to-fail experiment, even if it had not, we still would have learned how to do such an event better in the future or whether these types of activities did not work in communities like the one we manage.

Not everything is in our control. Ideally, we can adapt to setbacks and changes quickly and reconfigure our companies to better deal with the unknown.

Creativity and Imagination

In making your company more adaptable, creativity can be one of your greatest tools. Creativity and imagination can provide answers and ideas to address any issue. Dealing with change usually requires exploring new approaches. Brainstorming and asking for the views of people who might bring a fresh perspective can be helpful. Another way to unlock creativity is by taking the elements of a situation and playing with them. See how they could fit together differently to find a different configuration that will give you the result you want.

Picture an organization where one department is overburdened and not achieving the necessary results. The company's CEO could take the different components, such as the team, the systems and processes, the areas of responsibility, and the team's incentives, and determine the best mix. One answer might be to take one area of responsibility and give it to a different department where it may operate better.

I recently came across this type of situation. Our Finance manager was also managing our Corporate department. She has been a great performer in both roles, but she decided she wanted to focus on Finance only, as the position has been growing lately. I had to hire a new manager for our Corporate team.

Some tasks currently reside in our Corporate department, but they are better suited to our Finance manager's strengths, such as process management. I was worried about handing this responsibility to a new person. On the other hand, because we never had a fully formed Corporate team, there are some human resources-related processes in Finance that we moved back to Corporate. Playing with the different pieces of the department gave me room to make the transition as smooth as possible.

An additional way to use creativity in your problem-solving is to try looking at the entire picture from a different angle. What if you move the events forward or back in time? What happens when you change the actors? What happens when you change how they interact? Creativity is often about looking at a problem from a different perspective. By entering a playful mindset, you may see a whole new vision emerge that might provide a new clue.

Our brains use information from the past to solve new problems. If we find a problem with seemingly no solution, we reconstruct it to approach it similarly to a problem we have fixed before. To unlock other ways of looking at situations, we can use lateral thinking to find creative solutions.

The Trojan Horse is an example of this type of decision-making. The Greeks had been at war with the Trojans for ten years, unable to breach their walls or defenses. The typical assaults were not working. By reframing the problem, the Greeks decided to deceive the Trojans, which resulted in the desired outcome – versus finding a way to break down their barriers. The Greeks were able to finish the ten-year confrontation as a result of the Trojan Horse.[152]

Whenever I get stuck, I try to find colleagues I have worked with in the past to help me think of new ideas. I present my challenge, and we work together on different points of view. Finding experts on the topic and discussing ideas is also a way to move forward.

Working with other team members helps you come up with more creative ideas. For brainstorming to be effective, we must encourage people to bring their divergent ways of thinking, and everyone's views can then converge. If you do not follow the steps of this process, the team may converge prematurely. When one person presents an idea, that will prompt others to think similarly. On the other hand, if people have an opportunity to think on their own, they will find different ways to solve the same problem.

When I have used this exercise, I have not always implemented the ideas we came up with, but no matter what, I had a fuller understanding of the issue by the end of the discussion.

One technique that forces participants to diverge and then converge is called the 6-3-5. Six people sit together, and each one writes down three ideas. Everyone passes their group of approaches to the next person, who can then build their ideas on top of the other person's three original ones. The notes are passed around five times. The group then comes together to analyze the concepts—this process forces divergence and then convergence.[153]

Solving Problems in the Organization

Part of our job as business leaders is to face challenges: cumbersome work procedures, a product not selling as expected, or outright crises. For each challenge, there is a solution.

In his book, *The Beginning of Infinity*, David Deutsch shines a light on how we, as leaders, can approach this with optimism. "Optimism (in the sense that I have advocated) is the theory that all failures—all evils—are due to insufficient knowledge. . . . Problems are inevitable because our knowledge will always be infinitely far from complete."[154]

Although Deutsch points to the ubiquity of problems, he argues that we can address any "failure" or "evil" through information, which he describes as powerful. For any professional, knowledge is the key to solving the seemingly insurmountable.

That, according to Deutsch, is hopeful and optimistic: we can solve all problems through knowledge. It would be a mistake to equate complicated problems with issues for which we will never find a solution. "Problems are soluble," Deutsch writes, "and each particular evil is a problem that can be solved. An optimistic civilization is open and not afraid to innovate, and it is based on traditions of criticism.

Its institutions keep improving, and the most critical knowledge they embody is knowledge of how to detect and eliminate errors."[155]

In a way, our job as organizational leaders is to solve problems and prevent them from happening again. We are like engineers on a factory floor: if one of our machines stops working, we need to get our hands dirty and find out what happened. We may sometimes have to take the device apart to find the problem.

When faced with a problem, it is essential to diagnose what happened adequately before looking for solutions. It is easy to skip this step and go straight to a possible answer. On several occasions, I have had to pause a discussion in a meeting because we had too quickly moved into searching for solutions without first understanding what had gone wrong.

Wrong problem diagnosis is common in organizations. According to a survey of more than one hundred C-suite executives, 85 percent strongly agreed that their companies were deficient at diagnosing problems. Furthermore, 87 percent also strongly agreed that the lack of proper diagnosis came with high costs for the organization.[156]

Once you have detected a problem, you can find a suitable solution. Often, the problem is knotty and requires much trial and error. At this point, you may be tempted to give up and mark the situation as insoluble. Yet, there is always a solution. Once you have found it, your job is to make sure the problem never happens again.

Although David Deutsch refers to society's institutions, we can apply his definition of optimism to companies where our mandate as managers is to improve continuously. As leaders, we must make sure our companies become learning machines, which can find and resolve errors, grow, and adapt to their surrounding contexts.

For that to happen, your company must be open to knowledge, even if it shows that current processes are not working. Allowing information—even data that confronts deeply-held beliefs—to enter the company is one of the most challenging things to do. Accepting criticism and responding to it will lead your company to innovate, grow, and develop a culture of openness and problem-solving.

KEY TAKEAWAYS

- Our world's interconnectedness leads to the complex environment we inhabit. We can face five contexts: simple, complicated, complex, chaos, and disorder.

- Once we distinguish between these contexts, we can choose the right tools and management style for each situation.

- A complicated environment responds to cause and effect, but there may be more than one answer. A complex setting resides in the world of unknowns, where many factors are at play, and the results are unpredictable. When dealing with complexity, experimentation and empowered teams work better than rigid processes and trying to control actions and outcomes.

- In chaos, there are no patterns, and we must deal with the consequences of the situation. Disorder occurs when we are unclear which of the other settings predominates.

- We can also use systems theory when designing our companies. If we view our companies as living systems, we can better understand their current function and move in the desired direction.

- As part of our design, we can build plasticity-ready companies with the necessary resilience to recover from challenges without losing their ability to operate. Building resilience creates a trade-off with efficiency, but efficiency can give rise to rigid, brittle organizations.

- To promote plasticity, you can introduce diversity, empower autonomous management, link the company's units loosely, and encourage experimentation.

- To better understand our organizations, it is sometimes best to listen to what is happening. Other times we need more data before moving forward, and testing your environment is useful. Safe-to-fail experiments are controlled, scientific tests that will allow you to probe your circumstances so you can better understand your context. This new understanding, combined with creativity, can help us solve the problems we encounter.

Get Ahead, Stay Ahead

> Step-by-step, year-by-year, the world is improving. Not on every single measure every single year, but as a rule. Though the world faces huge challenges, we have made tremendous progress. This is the fact-based worldview.
>
> – Hans Rosling

Running a business successfully and making the best possible decisions depends on being aware of what is happening around you. Not only does your company evolve within itself, but it also does within its industry and in the world.

With the right team, the best structure, processes, and systems in place, you are in a position to take advantage of opportunities rather than merely being at the mercy of circumstances. Everyone in your industry faces the same uncertainties, so the changes around you can be sources of growth if you and your company seize those opportunities.

Being able to decipher an uncertain environment puts you at a competitive advantage. In times of constant change, we seek a respite through order—customers are drawn to organizations that operate well no matter what is happening around them. Your business will stand out to your customers if you make it an oasis where people are welcomed and know they will get what they need. They can feel at home and know that your company is where they can solve their problems.

Providing reliable service offers benefits. Customers who know they can rely on your business for guaranteed products and delivery will want to return.

UNDERSTANDING YOUR NICHE

Large, multinational companies have spent years refining their processes and communications to be responsive to their customers.

Small and medium-sized companies will have difficulty competing with those types of resources. More likely than not, if your firm is competitive, it is because you have found a niche.

In nature, species that have found niches thrive while others do not. The same is true for companies. For instance, in a market saturated with photographers, professionals who build photography businesses may wish to select a segment of that market. A photographer specializing in portraits of newborns will serve one type of client, while a wedding photographer serves others.

Similarly, not all technology development companies serve the same market. Some develop software for government agencies to help these types of organizations become efficient. As these technology companies become specialized in their niche, they learn from each additional client to better provide what their client needs and can deliver a better product than a company that has never competed in this segment.

The most successful companies are the ones that were able to find spaces where they can compete. There is an unlimited number of niches—the key is finding them, serving them, and building a protective moat around your company. Moats make companies more competitive and prosperous by defending their niches.

Charlie Munger and Warren Buffet recommend building the most substantial moat possible. Buffet explained this best in the 2000 Berkshire Hathaway annual meeting:

"So we think in terms of that moat and the ability to keep its width and its impossibility of being crossed as the primary criterion of a great business. And we tell our managers we want the moat widened every year. That doesn't necessarily mean profits will be larger this year than they were last year. However, if the moat is widened every year, the business will do very well. When we see a moat that's tenuous in any way—it's just too risky. We don't know how to evaluate that. And, therefore, we leave it alone. We think that all of our businesses—or virtually all of our businesses—have pretty darned good moats. And we think managers are widening them."[157]

Investment research firm Morningstar uses an economic moat rating to measure a company's competitive advantage. Their premise is that a company with a high score can earn higher returns on its capital and ward off competitors for many years.

According to Morningstar, some of the elements that give companies a wider moat are network effects (where an additional user adds value to other users of the product or service), intangible assets such as intellectual property and licenses, cost advantages (the ability to produce the product at lower costs), high switching costs (the cost move to use a different product), and economies of scale.[158]

Oracle, which produces software for companies, is an organization with a wide moat. Once a company has invested significant resources into implementing the software Oracle offers, it will be hesitant to switch companies again, as is our case. It took us longer than a year to implement our ERP. Every year, we program new enhancements to the information system—we are in it for the long run. Moving to a different software would imply more costs than I wish to consider.

Pharmaceutical companies that have valuable patents, such as Novartis, can also build more substantial moats. With the cash flows they receive from their royalties, they can develop more patents and increase their protections.

If we are successful in new, specialized markets, it is because no one else has solved the problems there before us. One way to improve our niches is to bring the best practices from other industries to these new spaces. Customers are instinctively drawn to a company that provides consistency and order, and they may even pay a premium for a reliable product. As you interact more and more with your customers, you will build that trust and grow together.

MAKING STRATEGY WORK

Operational excellence within your bit of jungle can also be a trigger for growth. If you can find ways to run your business within its industry smoothly, it can be the operational leader, bringing with it an edge over your competitors.

Operational excellence can be defined as a set of improvements organizations make to attain a competitive advantage.[159] Another way of achieving this, according to John Mitchell, author of *Operational Excellence: Journey to Creating Sustainable Value,* is to "safely create the greatest sustainable value." Although most companies see this as maximizing profit, shareholder value, or growth, value can differ from organization to organization. Reaching this goal is a journey to continuous improvement and constant progress to excellence.[160]

How well you consistently solve the problems and deal with the uncertainties your industry faces can provide a boost over time. Superior HR, recruiting programs, great systems/processes, and an overall culture of growth can lead to operational excellence. This underlying structure will translate into better products and higher returns over time.

We will continue to face new knots and messes or outright chaos. Problems can give you a chance to sharpen your operational machinery. The jungle is an opportunity where growth is just around the corner.

I recently received one of my favorite compliments during a conversation with one of our service providers, a real estate agent who sells our apartments and offices. She told me she trusted our company implicitly. She knew how our team manages the company, supported by its processes and systems, and she said she could rely on us to watch out for our common interests.

She mentioned that we had worked together for many years with no issues. Often, she will sell a unit before we have finished construction, sometimes many months in advance. Our policy is to pay commissions to real estate agents only when we have completed construction and have received the customer's final payment.

She recalled a commission payment we had to make after the initial sale of an office unit. She had forgotten all about that sale because we completed the building one year after we had signed the initial contract. Although we did not receive a bill from her, we called and asked her to pick up her check for the commission when we received the customer's final payment. We made the payment because it is a part of our process, and that is how we operate.

This vision is not idealistic and makes perfect business sense. As a client, I want to work with well-run, fair, and transparent companies. Potential and current clients, suppliers, and investors look for the same thing from my company and others. It is always a treat to work with an institution that treats people well. Once you build the relationship and grow to trust each other, a sense of mutual goodwill emerges. Little quirks are easily pardoned, and there is room to develop ample relationships that work over the long run.

Becoming an oasis for others depends on how you configure your company. The elements will not vary. It takes a great team of people committed to the company's mission. It also takes weaving reliability into the culture, where everybody works hard to keep promises. An excellent infrastructure and its underlying systems and processes, the first three pillars of Heptagram, ensure that you encode the ethos of responsiveness and organization in the firm. A firm can always learn from past mistakes or find new ways to innovate. The final ingredient is constant improvement, working tirelessly to be dynamic, responsive, and effective.

You may not realize when your company becomes an oasis of organization—though occasional compliments may hint at what you have achieved. Another clue is that avoidable problems will have diminished. I received praise about our company from one of our service providers while she was in the middle of complaining about one of our policies. She contrasted this policy with how well-run she felt the organization was overall. We took her feedback into account and are modifying that policy. Our goal is to continually improve our organization and make it what we idealistically see as a well-run, responsive company.

The University of Utah gives out the Shingo Prize for Operational Excellence. It was initially named the Shingo Prize for Excellence in Manufacturing in 1988. According to Robert Miller, Executive Director for the prize, the Shingo Prize is based on the Shingo Model, whose standard for operational excellence is the "most rigorous in the world."[161]

The Shingo Model asserts that operational excellence depends on continuous process improvement with a goal toward perfection. We all know we will never attain perfection, but the search for it pushes us to get to where we have not been in the past.

The way to go about this is to look for problems, even in places where none are apparent. The thinking goes that doing this will drive improvement. Looking in non-obvious places opens new challenges, and a relentless push for progress will lift operations and create better products for your customers.[162]

The Shingo Model describes a few ways to bolster the search for continuous improvement. Processes, for example, need to be standardized, so they need less supervision, and the work itself will show that procedures are being followed.

Standardized processes guarantee that improvement is institutionalized and prevent the company from slipping back to its old ways of doing things. With managers spending less time supervising the work, they are free to work on other improvements, which cascades out to more refinements that are added to standardized processes, ensuring that the growth is maintained.

A positive side effect of continuous improvement is the reduction of waste. Anything that becomes an obstacle to a workflow is a loss— whether that means time or physical resources. Getting rid of waste is easily understood, and everyone associated with the process can play a role in this. Too often, with improvements, we focus on growth and added value, but eliminating any waste is also productive.

The more organic the pursuit for improvement is, the more sustainable it will be, and it will lead to fresher ideas for the company's overall continuous evolution.[163]

One of my favorite examples of our development at Celaque is related to our hiring process. In the beginning, it involved a short checklist of primary steps, such as receiving and selecting resumes, interviewing candidates, and then selecting an applicant. We sought to improve our hiring process continuously, so we kept questioning how we were doing everything, and therefore, our procedure continued to evolve.

When we analyzed our procedures, we realized that sifting through resumes was very time-consuming, and it was a step that we could improve. We added a questionnaire that supplies standard answers, some of which we would not ordinarily find on a person's resume. This form saved us valuable hours of work by helping us eliminate candidates who were unsuited for the position at hand.

We also polished the rest of our process. We realized we needed to use different types of interviews, so we added structured interview questions. Then, instead of one or two people making the final decision, we put in a concluding meeting where we included four people in a committee-based choice.

We have continued to improve our hiring process. This constant search has also pushed us to research other companies' best practices and adopt those that could work for us.

THRIVING IN CHAOS

If your company is well structured and work is flowing smoothly, you will be able to see opportunities as they arrive. Otherwise, the value of some ideas may not be apparent at first glance.

New business opportunities are all around us, and new solutions are emerging all the time. One way to identify them is to locate emerging ideas that have not been organized for customers yet and pursue ways to package and sell them. You can study the fringes of your industry in newly developing areas to find additional avenues for growth.

Charlie Munger and Warren Buffet recommend understanding your "circle of competence" and not moving beyond it.[164] The idea is that we all have areas of expertise based on our education and experience. As we progress in our careers and spend more time learning about the world, we increase our fields of competence, giving ourselves more space to compete.

No matter how much we expand, we cannot be experts in everything. When Alianza started, we began by selling office space, and we did so for a few years until we decided to expand into the leasing of office space. We saw that many customers were looking to lease ample, competitively priced office space. We then moved into leasing smaller spaces and experimented with different types of contracts such as leasing with an option to buy, short-term leases, and leasing furnished office spaces.

Building owners began to form associations to manage their properties, and our customers frequently asked us to maintain the buildings we had developed. Once we started leasing, we recognized the parallels between that business and managing a building, and that is how we expanded into operating the buildings we developed.

The market for office space in Tegucigalpa is not unlimited, so we had to find other types of markets, leading us to residential buildings. We started with higher-priced apartments in prime locations. At Alianza, we developed two locations with more than 190 apartments, and at Celaque, we built one with 138 apartments. Now, we sell, lease, and manage the units in these buildings.

We are also expanding our product line in areas adjacent to the markets we know best. We built more economically-priced apartments in less-centric locations. By moving into new types of buildings, we add more services that become part of our income streams.

As we expand our circle of competence, we learn. We did not go into managing buildings knowing everything, but we had the infrastructure to properly maintain the premises because we had procured each building's components during the construction process. Also, our leasing operations gave us the management know-how, and we knew our clients because we had sold or leased the space to them. Managing buildings prompted us to combine our competencies in new ways.

Seizing new opportunities only occurs when you make time and space for them. Once our companies are operating well, we will naturally have more room to find new areas for growth. Warren Buffet famously spends his time poring over information.[165] His job is to think. His accumulation of knowledge leads him to new investment opportunities.

The world is constantly in motion. The more dynamic our organizations are, the more we will be able to take advantage of new areas for growth as they arise. As the company continues to evolve, it will learn how to launch new ideas, becoming a self-reinforcing muscle.

KEY TAKEAWAYS

- The most successful companies are ones that can find spaces where they can compete. There is an unlimited number of niches—the key is finding them, serving them, and building a protective moat around your company.

- Continuous operational excellence can be achieved through standardized processes, reducing waste, and a constant search for progress.

- New business opportunities are all around us, and new solutions are emerging all the time. If your company is well structured and work is flowing smoothly, you will be able to see opportunities as they appear and take advantage of them.

Conclusion

The point isn't to be the hero and solve things; the point of the leader in a complex world is to enable and unleash as many heroes and as many solutions as possible.

– Jennifer Garvey Berger

The COVID-19 pandemic forced us to shut down our construction sites and move the rest of our operations to remote work. We all had to make personal adjustments to our lifestyles. I retreated to working from home and homeschooling three girls aged four, six, and eight. To say it was a period of intense activity is an understatement. Yet, the crisis had its silver linings. We found new business opportunities during that period, and we had the time to enhance our structure and operations to a level we had never attained before.

I never imagined when I was writing the book or building Celaque that we would have to deal with an unprecedented disruption to our health systems and our economies. Interestingly, though, perhaps because of my background, I am always ready for a crisis, and without realizing it, I created the blueprint for Celaque with that in mind. As presented in this book, the Heptagram model reflects that consciousness, which played a big role in facilitating our company's seamless transition during the pandemic.

We have a great team, and they were able to harness our company infrastructure to continue working as before (only in different locations)—those in our group whose typical responsibilities are presence-based transitioned into other teams. We also took the extra energy and time to develop a creative team to look for new income streams during this complex situation.

The seven pillars of Heptagram kept us towering high over the chaos that surrounded us. Our organizational configuration, systems, and processes all worked and helped us maintain a sense of normalcy.

We continued working where we could. Even though we had to pause our construction activities for some weeks, we did not stop developing current and new projects so that we could be ready for when we could all go out again.

NOISE AND OPPORTUNITY

We are fortunate because we have more opportunities than any generation before us. We have more income, more education, and better health,[166] and we also have access to the knowledge of our ancestors, plus all the wisdom of contemporary thinkers.

Our challenge is figuring out how to take that legacy and put it to good use, so our organizations can reach their full potential. Even more important, how do we better understand the world we live in and recognize new opportunities we might not otherwise have seen? We live in a different world than our parents and grandparents inhabited, which means we are also traveling in uncharted territory. A lot of what we studied during our formal educations has been superseded by new information.

Learning from the past is important because we are standing on very tall shoulders, dating back to the ancients. Lessons are everywhere, and each new step of learning builds on the prior one. Mastering the basics, such as the teachings of Frederick Taylor and other thinkers, can give us the right tools at the right time instead of relying on a single answer for everything. The more we know about our history, the more tools we will have at our fingertips, and the better we will be able to respond to disrupting events.

The present also has valuable lessons. Our interactions with clients, suppliers, and colleagues, our study of current management trends, what we learn about how other companies have solved problems—there is much to take in. As we take the time to listen, we can distinguish between what is essential and what is just noise.

YOUR TURN

Our primary task is to structure our organizations in the best way possible. This work includes selecting the right organizational structures, designing efficient processes, and finding the best team we can.

As you design your company, start by looking at the first pillar in the Heptagram model: your organizational structure. Ask yourself which configuration works best for your organization. If you already have the right structure, you might want to reassess how each team is configured and whether the roles and responsibilities are in the best places. A company's architecture is a continuous work in process, as we have learned at Celaque.

Information systems and processes govern how work is operated in a company. The more robust your processes are, the better your company will adapt to changing circumstances. I recommend implementing the best information systems you can afford to support your operations fully.

Customized metrics for your company will help you know how well it is operating. They will also point to problems in your workflows, including how you and your team manage your processes and possible gaps in the information systems you are using. Metrics will point to areas for growth and potential new products.

As leaders of companies, we must face the unknowable and the complex. In places where the work is knowable, a more ordered approach for most of the company's operations will make them more efficient and will make it more likely to reach the results it seeks.[167] Vital mechanisms for ensuring consistency and quality are processes, policies, metrics, and information systems. They make up the company's infrastructure.

Without reliable support, it is difficult to achieve anything else. How well we set up the framework and how well it works determines how competitive the company can be. This arrangement can be thorough yet light, geared to results yet adaptable, and simple. With a sound base, you will provide the product that your customers want while efficiently and effectively using the company's available resources

Continue to tweak and make changes every year to ensure your workflows stay current with your present reality. Never forget that Heptagram will only work if you use it as the dynamic foundation of a very complex organism. What I have tried to create is a highly adaptable system that can encompass any necessary adjustments. This, I believe, is the method's biggest strength.

Our companies are systems, organisms that are bigger than the sum of their parts. They require plasticity to adapt to their environments, which are constantly changing. As leaders, we can develop the tools to better communicate and establish trusting environments within our organizations. We can also design our companies to be resilient and capable of responding to different circumstances, whether they are complex, confusing, or even chaotic.

Not everything needs to be systematized and made to be as efficient as possible. Space for self-organization and redundancy is valuable because it makes the company more resilient. The balance is delicate and needs regular adjustment. A certain level of organization is fundamental and inefficient workflows need to be constantly put to the test and redesigned.

A company's structure usually has an inherent tension. Too much bureaucracy will thwart creativity and dynamism. Too much flexibility will cause mistakes to accumulate. Processes are the answer for ensuring that a certain level of quality is consistently maintained, but with too many procedures, your operation may become too machine-like. Allowing self-organization and inventiveness to emerge within a business can promote breakthroughs that otherwise would have been impossible. However, too relaxed a structure can invite chaos and angry customers.

Each company's balance is unique. The combination of structure, emergence, and flexibility that best suits an organization resides along a multi-dimensional continuum reflected in the Heptagram concept. Flexible lines bind together the seven pillars, one may tighten while others relax, but a certain balance is always maintained. Some companies may thrive on a higher dose of freedom, while others require a more balanced mixture. The right blend is based on its goals, how its teams work together, and what it produces.

This mix may change as the company evolves. A looser organization will probably be more critical when it is a startup, but it will have to include more structure as it starts to have more transactions and grows. Too many processes might be a problem. As Eric Schmidt and Jonathan Rosenberg suggest in *How Google Works*, procedures will always be behind a company's growth: "The business should always be outrunning the processes, so chaos is right where you want to be."[168]

We can build self-learning companies that leverage all the knowledge within the organization and enable virtuous cycles of learning. In the end, we live in a world that continually changes, and we must create adaptable systems that will be able to evolve and even thrive in these uncertain circumstances.

Our work at Celaque continues. We are always tweaking, adapting, and improving. Some phases are more difficult than others, but we profit from times of uncertainty to revise our workflows and structure to come out stronger on the other side. As we evolve as an organization, we continue to grow as a real estate developer. We have more projects in our pipeline than ever before, and we are committed to creating beautiful buildings that enrich people's lives.

Counting on a proven method like Heptagram is important to get the ball rolling. It is an open system that is now in your hands. The result of many years of hard work and trial and error, this seven-pillar model has helped me build and expand a thriving business, and I cannot wait to see what other passionate and talented entrepreneurs will do with it. An open system is a work-in-progress, and now it is your turn to contribute to it.

We are lucky to be living in this time and age. Along with the chaotic cacophony of the modern world come endless opportunities. As we all navigate our ever-changing circumstances, I hope you will adapt the Heptagram model to fit your business and context. My highest aspiration is that the discoveries described in this book will help you build great companies to improve our world.

Acknowledgments

I want to acknowledge every person that made this book possible. To my incredible assistant, Violeta Vasilopoulou, I cannot thank you enough. You helped me through this process from beginning to end and have become a true friend.

To my editing team, which included Henry Ferris and Veronica Pamoukaghlian, it felt like you took me through a master's degree in writing. I love how the book turned out. To Ma Victoria Acuña, my gratitude for your help in researching hundreds of papers. Thank you, Fredrik Hacklin, for reviewing my book from an academic perspective, Peggy McColl for your indomitable positivity, and Happy Self Publishing for creating this beautiful book.

My special gratitude goes to my Master Mind group—Mireya Nasser, Danielle Kluck, and Andrea Chang. Your support through all my crazy ideas helped me bring this book to the light of day.

I say gracias to everyone at Celaque for your patience as I tried idea after idea in our company's laboratory. You are the best team I could ever imagine.

My endless gratitude to my family and friends for your support throughout the journey of writing and publishing this book. Thank you for listening to me and for contributing to the book in a million different ways.

To my mom, Diana, and my dad, Tomas, thank you for life, the greatest gift. I love you both forever.

Alicia, Abigail, and Amanda: you are the reason behind everything I do. Thank you for helping mommy make her dream of writing a book come true.

José, my husband and greatest champion, you have been with me every step of the way. Thank you for listening to me when I felt stuck or lost and for helping me move forward, always. I could not have done this without you. I love you.

About the Author

Pamela Ayuso is an entrepreneur and writer. A real estate developer with over a decade of executive leadership experience in real estate, Pamela is the CEO and co-founder of Celaque.

Celaque, a multimillion-dollar company, develops office and residential buildings in Honduras and manages a broad portfolio of properties. Pamela's focus is on growing Celaque into a model for the 21st-century company.

Pamela earned a Bachelor of Science degree, summa cum laude, in finance and accounting from Ithaca College and a Master of International Affairs, specializing in international finance, from Columbia University. She is a Certified Public Accountant (CPA) in the State of New York.

She is an avid reader and writer interested in sharing her journey as a business leader through writing. Her blog helps other entrepreneurs build their businesses. Pamela has written on diverse topics like 'Creating Your Teams for a Successful Company,' 'The Importance of Building Resilience into Your Company,' and many others for business leaders.

She is also the author of two children's books: Alicia and Bunnie Paint a Mural and the upcoming Amanda and Sophia's Adventures in the Forest, both inspired by her daughters.

Pamela splits her time between the city and the country with her husband and three daughters. She loves to paint and, since the pandemic, has discovered cooking and baking.

You can stay connected with her at www.pamelaayuso.com.

Connect with the Author

Instagram:
https://www.instagram.com/pamelaayuso

LinkedIn:
https://www.linkedin.com/in/pamelaayuso

Facebook:
https://www.facebook.com/pamelaayuso

Twitter:
https://twitter.com/pamelaayuso

Keep Learning

Keep learning and building your company with Heptagram.

Please visit www.pamelaayuso.com/heptagram-bonus to download our:

- Heptagram Workbook
- Heptagram Checklists

And learn about updates and programs associated with Heptagram.

Leave a Review

If you enjoyed this book, please write a review on the retail site where you bought this book. Your review will make this book more visible to new readers. I appreciate your feedback and would love to hear your thoughts.

Thank you for reading my book!
Pamela

Notes

1. Jay R. Galbraith, *Designing Organizations: Strategy, Structure, and Process at the Business Unit and Enterprise Levels*, third edition, The Jossey-Bass Business & Management Series (San Francisco: Jossey-Bass, 2014), 37-38.

2. Vivek Sehgal, *Supply Chain As Strategic Asset: The Key to Reaching Business Goals*, first edition, Wiley Corporate F&A (Hoboken, N.J.: Wiley, 2011), 148.

3. Mu-Jeung Yang, Lorenz Kueng, and Bryan Hong, "Business Strategy and the Management of Firms," *NBER Working Papers* (National Bureau of Economic Research, Inc, January 2015), https://ideas.repec.org/p/nbr/nberwo/20846.html.

4. Galbraith, *Designing Organizations,* 20.

5. Richard M. Burton, Børge Obel, and Dorthe Døjbak Håkonsson, *Organizational Design: A Step-by-Step Approach*, third edition (Cambridge University Press, 2015), 69.

6. Galbraith, *Designing Organizations,* 23-24.

7. D. Harold Doty, William H. Glick, and George P. Huber, "Fit, Equifinality, and Organizational Effectiveness: A Test of Two Configurational Theories," *The Academy of Management Journal* 36, no. 6 (1993): 1196–1250, https://doi.org/10.2307/256810.

8. Richard M. Burton, Jørgen Lauridsen, and Børge Obel, "Return on Assets Loss from Situational and Contingency Misfits." *Management Science* 48, no. 11 (November 2002): 1461–85, https://doi.org/10.1287/mnsc.48.11.1461.262. AND Henk W. Volberda et al., "Contingency Fit, Institutional Fit, and Firm Performance: A Metafit Approach to Organization-Environment Relationships," *Organization Science* 23, no. 4 (August 7, 2012): 1040–54, https://doi.org/10.1287/orsc.1110.0687.

9. Burton, Obel, and Håkonsson, *Organizational Design,* 7.

10. Burton, Obel, and Håkonsson, *Organizational Design,* 71.

11. Burton, Obel, and Håkonsson, *Organizational Design*, 71.

12. Burton, Obel, and Håkonsson, *Organizational Design*, 69-94.

13. Galbraith, *Designing Organizations*, 26.

14. Eric Schmidt, Alan Eagle, and Jonathan Rosenberg, *How Google Works*, first edition (New York, NY: Grand Central Publishing, 2014), 43-44.

15. Burton, Obel, and Håkonsson, *Organizational Design*, 69-94.

16. Burton, Obel, and Håkonsson, *Organizational Design*, 69-94.

17. Schmidt, Eagle, and Rosenberg, *How Google Works*, 44.

18. Burton, Obel, and Håkonsson, *Organizational Design*, 69-94.

19. Galbraith, *Designing Organizations*, 27.

20. Burton, Obel, and Håkonsson, *Organizational Design*, 69-94.

21. Linn C Stuckenbruck, "The Matrix Organization," *Project Management Quarterly* 10, no. 3 (1979): 21–33.

22. Stanley M. Davis and Paul R. Lawrence, "Problems of Matrix Organizations." *Harvard Business Review* 56, no. 3 (June 5, 1978): 131–42.

23. Herman Vantrappen and Frederic Wirtz, "Making Matrix Organizations Actually Work." *Harvard Business Review Digital Articles*, (March 01, 2016), 2–5.

24. Galbraith, *Designing Organizations*, 35.

25. Galbraith, *Designing Organizations*, 65-66.

26. Vantrappen and Wirtz, "Making Matrix Organizations Actually Work."

27. Vantrappen and Wirtz, "Making Matrix Organizations Actually Work."

28. Galbraith, *Designing Organizations*, 38.

29. Ann Majchrzak and Qianwei Wang, "Breaking the Functional Mind-Set in Process Organizations." *Harvard Business Review* 74, no. 5 (October 9, 1996), 93–99.

30. Ron Ashkenas, "Jack Welch's Approach to Breaking Down Silos Still Works." *Harvard Business Review Digital Articles* (September 9, 2015), 2–4.

31. Vantrappen and Wirtz, "Making Matrix Organizations Actually Work."

32. Vantrappen and Wirtz, "Making Matrix Organizations Actually Work."

33. Schmidt, Eagle, and Rosenberg, *How Google Works*, 175-176.

34. Stanley A. McChrystal et al., *Team of Teams: New Rules of Engagement for a Complex World* (New York, New York: Portfolio/Penguin, 2015), 151.

35. Galbraith, *Designing Organizations*, 40.

36. Klara Palmberg, "Exploring Process Management: Are There Any Widespread Models and Definitions?" *TQM Journal* 21, no. 2 (May 2009), 203–15.

37. Sergey Smirnov et al., "Business Process Model Abstraction: A Definition, Catalog, and Survey." *Distributed and Parallel Databases* 30, no. 1 (February 1, 2012), 63–99, https://doi.org/10.1007/s10619-011-7088-5.

38. Galbraith, *Designing Organizations*, 38-40.

39. Charles Duhigg, *The Power of Habit: Why We Do What We Do in Life and Business*, Concentrated Knowledge for the Busy Executive, second edition (Kennett Square, PA: Random House, 2012), 17-18.

40. Ayelet Fishbach, "How to Keep Working When You're Just Not Feeling It: Four Strategies for Motivating Yourself." *Harvard Business Review* 96, no 6 (2018), 138-141.

41. Adam M. Grant, "Employees without a Cause: The Motivational Effects of Prosocial Impact in Public Service." *International Public Management Journal* 11, no. 1 (April 2008), 48–66, https://doi.org/10.1080/10967490801887905.

42. Deborah A. Small and George Loewenstein, "Helping a Victim or Helping the Victim: Altruism and Identifiability.," *Journal of Risk & Uncertainty* 26, no. 1 (January 2003), 5–16, https://doi.org/10.1023/A:1022299422219.

43. Robert A. Karasek, "Job Demands, Job Decision Latitude, and Mental Strain: Implications for Job Redesign." *Administrative Science Quarterly* 24, no. 2 (1979), 285–308, https://doi.org/10.2307/2392498.

44. Atul Gawande, *The Checklist Manifesto: How to Get Things Right*, 1st edition (New York: Metropolitan Books, 2009), 120.

45. Ann Lindsay, Denise Downs, and Ken Lunn, "Business Processes— Attempts to Find a Definition." *Information and Software Technology* 45, no. 15 (January 1, 2003), 1015–19, https://doi.org/10.1016/S0950-5849(03)00129-0.

46. K. Sugitani and H. Morita, "The Approach for Skill up in Five-Why for Investigating Root Cause of Quality Problems." *International Journal of Data Analysis Techniques and Strategies* 3, no. 3 (2011), 221–40, https://doi.org/10.1504/IJDATS.2011.041332.

47. Olivier Serrat, "The Five Whys Technique." *International Publications*, February 1, 2009, https://digitalcommons.ilr.cornell.edu/intl/198.

48. Bonnie Collier and Tom DeMarco, "A Defined Process for Project Postmortem Review." *IEEE Software* 13, no. 4 (July 1996), 65, https://doi.org/10.1109/52.526833.

49. Galbraith, *Designing Organizations,* 40.

50. Yaser Hasan Salem Al-Mamary, Alina Shamsuddin, and A.H. Nor Aziati, "The Role of Different Types of Information Systems In Business Organizations : A Review." *International Journal of Research* 1, no. 7 (August 5, 2014), 1279–86.

51. Deepak Kumar and Anita Bhatia, "Role of IT in Business Process Reengineering," in *2011 International Conference on Recent Trends in Information Systems, ReTIS 2011 - Proceedings* (2011), 48–51, https://doi.org/10.1109/ReTIS.2011.6146838.

52. Gian Luca Petruzzi and A. Claudio Garavelli, "The Strategic Value of the 'Fit' between Business Processes and IT Management: The Case of the Italian Publishing Industry," in *2007 2nd IEEE/IFIP International Workshop on Business-Driven IT Management* (2007), 110–11, https://doi.org/10.1109/BDIM.2007.375021.

53. Ray Dalio, *Principles: Life and Work*, (New York: Simon & Schuster, 2017), 451-452.

54. David Parmenter, *Key Performance Indicators : Developing, Implementing, and Using Winning KPIs.*, third edition. (Hoboken, N.J.: Wiley, 2007), xv- xviii.

55. Parmenter, *Key Performance Indicators: Developing, Implementing, and Using Winning KPIs*, 11-15.

56. Shane E. Brown and Andrew J. Steger, "Key Performance Indicators Are Not Just About Profit | CFMA," *CFMA Building Profits* (April 2013), https://s3.amazonaws.com/rdcms-cfma/files/production/public/MABP13%20Brown%20Steger%20Eprint_72.pdf.

57. Harold Kerzner, "Key Performance Indicators." in *Project Management Metrics, KPIs, and Dashboards: A Guide to Measuring and Monitoring Project Performance*, second edition (Hoboken, New Jersey: Wiley, 2013), 448.

58. Brown and Steger, "Key Performance Indicators Are Not Just About Profit | CFMA."

59. Kerzner, "Key Performance Indicators."

60. Parmenter, *Key Performance Indicators: Developing, Implementing, and Using Winning KPIs*, 13-14.

61. Michael J. Mauboussin, "The True Measures of Success." *Harvard Business Review* 90, no. 10 (October 2012), 46–56.

62. Daniel Kahneman, *Thinking, Fast and Slow.*, first edition (New York: Farrar, Straus and Giroux, 2011), 262.

63. Kahneman, *Thinking, Fast and Slow*, 130.

64. Kahneman, *Thinking, Fast and Slow*, 292.

65. Dalio, Principles: *Life and Work*, 452.

66. Mauboussin, "The True Measures of Success."

67. Mauboussin, "The True Measures of Success."

68. Mauboussin, "The True Measures of Success."

69. Parmenter, *Key Performance Indicators: Developing, Implementing, and Using Winning KPIs*, 19-21.

70. Linda J. Popky, "Identify the Marketing Metrics That Actually Matter." *Harvard Business Review Digital Articles* (July 14, 2015), 2–4.

71. Dalio, Principles: *Life and Work*, 452.

72. Paul P. Baard, Edward L. Deci, and Richard M. Ryan, "Intrinsic Need Satisfaction: A Motivational Basis of Performance and Well-Being Two Work Settings." *Journal of Applied Social Psychology* 34, no. 10 (October 2004), 2045–68, https://doi.org/10.1111/j.1559-1816.2004.tb02690.x.

73. Dan N. Stone, Edward L. Deci, and Richard M. Ryan, "Beyond Talk: Creating Autonomous Motivation through Self-Determination Theory." *Journal of General Management* 34, no. 3 (2009), 75–91, https://doi.org/10.1177/030630700903400305.

74. Robert F. Hurley, "The Decision to Trust." *Harvard Business Review* 84, no. 9 (September 2006), 55–62.

75. J. David Lewis and Andrew Weigert, "Trust as a Social Reality." *Social Forces* 63, no. 4 (June 1985), 967–85, https://doi.org/10.2307/2578601.

76. Ronald S. Burt and Marc Knez, "Trust and Third-Party Gossip," in *Trust in Organizations: Frontiers of Theory and Research* (Thousand Oaks, Calif: SAGE Publications, Inc., 1996), 68–89, https://doi.org/10.4135/9781452243610.

77. Lewis and Weigert, "Trust as a Social Reality."

78. Peter D. Kaufman, *Poor Charlie's Almanack: The Wit and Wisdom of Charles T. Munger*, expanded third edition (Walsworth Publishing Company, 2005), 466.

79. Adnan Ozyilmaz, Berrin Erdogan, and Aysegul Karaeminogullari, "Trust in Organization as a Moderator of the Relationship between Self-efficacy and Workplace Outcomes: A Social Cognitive Theory-based Examination." *Journal of Occupational & Organizational Psychology* 91, no. 1 (March 2018), 181–204, https://doi.org/10.1111/joop.12189.

80. Holly Henderson Brower, Scott Wayne Lester, and M. Audrey Korsgaard, "Want Your Employees to Trust You? Show You Trust Them." *Harvard Business Review Digital Articles* (July 5, 2017), 2–5.

81. Marita Heyns and Sebastiaan Rothmann, "Volitional Trust, Autonomy Satisfaction, and Engagement at Work." *Psychological Reports* 121, no. 1 (February 2018), 112–34, https://doi.org/10.1177/0033294117718555.

82. Heyns and Rothmann, "Volitional Trust, Autonomy Satisfaction, and Engagement at Work."

83. Nurullah Gur and Christian Bjørnskov, "Trust and Delegation: Theory and Evidence." *Journal of Comparative Economics* 45, no. 3 (August 1, 2017), 644–57, https://doi.org/10.1016/j.jce.2016.02.002.

84. Heyns and Rothmann, "Volitional Trust, Autonomy Satisfaction, and Engagement at Work."

85. Richard Lewis, "Peter Kaufman on The Multidisciplinary Approach to Thinking: Transcript." *Latticework Investing* (April 06, 2018), http://latticeworkinvesting.com/2018/04/06/peter-kaufman-on-the-multidisciplinary-approach-to-thinking/.

86. Deborah Ancona and Kate Isaacs, "How to Give Your Team the Right Amount of Autonomy." *Harvard Business Review Digital Articles* (July 11, 2019), 2–4.

87. Brower, Lester, and Korsgaard, "Want Your Employees to Trust You? Show You Trust Them."

88. Brower, Lester, and Korsgaard, "Want Your Employees to Trust You? Show You Trust Them."

89. Heyns and Rothmann, "Volitional Trust, Autonomy Satisfaction, and Engagement at Work."

90. Heyns and Rothmann, "Volitional Trust, Autonomy Satisfaction, and Engagement at Work."

91. Kaufman, *Poor Charlie's Almanack*, 490-491.

92. Ozyilmaz, Erdogan, and Karaeminogullari, "Trust in Organization as a Moderator of the Relationship between Self-efficacy and Workplace Outcomes."

93. S. Duane Hansen, Benjamin B. Dunford, Alan D.Boss, R.Wayne Boss, and Ingo Angermeier, "Corporate Social Responsibility and the Benefits of Employee Trust: A Cross-Disciplinary Perspective." *Journal of Business Ethics* 102, no. 1 (January 2011), 29–45, https://doi.org/10.1007/s10551-011-0903-0.

94. Lewis and Weigert, "Trust as a Social Reality."

95. Ancona and Isaacs, "How to Give Your Team the Right Amount of Autonomy."

96. Burt and Knez, "Trust and Third-Party Gossip."

97. Brower, Lester, and Korsgaard, "Want Your Employees to Trust You? Show You Trust Them."

98. Schmidt, Eagle, and Rosenberg, *How Google Works*, 5, 176, 181.

99. Alice Grey Harrison, "Engagement Ring: Building Connections between Employees and Strategy." *Public Relations Tactics* 20, no. 5 (May 2013), 16.

100. Francesca Gino, "How to Make Employees Feel Like They Own Their Work." *Harvard Business Review Digital Articles* (December 7, 2015), 2–5.

101. Schmidt, Eagle, and Rosenberg, *How Google Works*, 54.

102. Paul Leinwand, Cesare Mainardi, and Art Kleiner, "Develop Your Company's Cross-Functional Capabilities." *Harvard Business Review Digital Articles* (February 2, 2016), 2–6.

103. Paul Gompers and Silpa Kovvali, "The Other Diversity Dividend." *Harvard Business Review* 96, no. 4 (August 7, 2018), 72–77.

104. Behnam Tabrizi, "75% of Cross-Functional Teams Are Dysfunctional." *Harvard Business Review Digital Articles* (June 23, 2015), 2–4.

105. Tom Krattemnaker, "Make Every Meeting Matter." *Harvard Management Update* 12, no. 12 (December 2007), 3–5.

106. Krattemnaker, "Make Every Meeting Matter."

107. Dana Rousmaniere, "What Everyone Needs to Know About Running Productive Meetings." *Harvard Business Review Digital Articles* (March 13, 2015), 2–5.

108. Ikujiro Nonaka, "The Knowledge-Creating Company." *Harvard Business Review* (July 1, 2007), https://hbr.org/2007/07/the-knowledge-creating-company.

109. Nonaka, "The Knowledge-Creating Company."

110. Nonaka, "The Knowledge-Creating Company."

111. César A. Hidalgo, *Why Information Grows: The Evolution of Order, From Atoms to Economies* (New York, New York: Basic Books, 2015), 66.

112. Edwin A. Locke and Gary P. Latham, "Building a Practically Useful Theory of Goal Setting and Task Motivation: A 35-Year Odyssey." *American Psychologist* 57, no. 9 (2002): 705–17, https://doi.org/10.1037/0003-066X.57.9.705. AND Dick Grote, "3 Popular Goal-Setting Techniques Managers Should Avoid." *Harvard Business Review Digital Articles* (January 2, 2017), 2–5.

113. Vanessa Hill and Harry Van Buren, "Taylor Won: The Triumph of Scientific Management and Its Meaning for Business and Society," in *Business and Society 360*, ed. James Weber and David M. Wasieleski, vol. 2 (Emerald Publishing Limited, 2018), 265–94, https://doi.org/10.1108/S2514-175920180000002007.

114. Hindy Lauer Schachter, "The Role Played by Frederick Taylor in the Rise of the Academic Management Fields," ed. Joyce Heames, *Journal of Management History* 16, no. 4 (September 28, 2010), 437–48, https://doi.org/10.1108/17511341011073924.

115. Sonia Taneja, Mildred Golden Pryor, and Leslie A. Toombs, "Frederick W. Taylor's Scientific Management Principles: Relevance and Validity." *Journal of Applied Management and Entrepreneurship* 16, no. 3 (June 2011), 60–78.

116. Lauer Schachter, "The Role Played by Frederick Taylor in the Rise of the Academic Management Fields."

117. Frederick Winslow Taylor, *The Principles of Scientific Management* (New York: Harper & Brothers, 1911), 64.

118. Jean Chanaron and Jacques Perrin, "Science, Technology and Work Organization." *International Journal of Technology Management* 2 (May 1, 1987), 377–89, https://doi.org/10.1504/IJTM.1987.026135.

119. Lauer Schachter, "The Role Played by Frederick Taylor in the Rise of the Academic Management Fields."

120. David M. Savino, "Frederick Winslow Taylor and His Lasting Legacy of Functional Leadership Competence." *Journal of Leadership, Accountability & Ethics* 13, no. 1 (March 2016), 70–76.

121. Taneja, Pryor, and Toombs, "Frederick W. Taylor's Scientific Management Principles."

122. Savino, "Frederick Winslow Taylor and His Lasting Legacy of Functional Leadership Competence."

123. Joseph R. Fiksel, *Resilient by Design: Creating Businesses That Adapt and Flourish in a Changing World* (Washington: Island Press, 2015), 3.

124. Adam B. Smith, "2018's Billion Dollar Disasters in Context." *NOAA Climate.gov*, February 7, 2019, https://www.climate.gov/news-features/blogs/beyond-data/2018s-billion-dollar-disasters-context.

125. Wen-Hsien Chen, "Business Process Management: A Thermodynamics Perspective." *Journal of Applied Management Studies* 8, no.2 (December 1999), 241.

126. David J. Snowden and Mary E. Boone, "A Leader's Framework for Decision Making." *Harvard Business Review* 85, no. 11 (2007), 69–76.

127. Dalio, *Principles: Life and Work,* 61.

128. Dalio, *Principles: Life and Work,* 543.

129. Snowden and Boone, "A Leader's Framework for Decision Making."

130. Snowden and Boone, "A Leader's Framework for Decision Making."

131. Snowden and Boone, "A Leader's Framework for Decision Making."

132. Snowden and Boone, "A Leader's Framework for Decision Making."

133. Donella H. Meadows and Diana Wright, *Thinking in Systems: A Primer* (White River Junction, VT: Chelsea Green Pub, 2008), 11-12.

134. Meadows and Wright, *Thinking in Systems*, 15.

135. "Resilience | Meaning of Resilience by Lexico," Lexico Dictionaries (accessed December 23, 2019), https://www.lexico.com/definition/resilience.

136. Brian H. Walker and David Salt, *Resilience Thinking: Sustaining Ecosystems and People in a Changing World* (Washington, DC: Island Press, 2006), chap. 3, Kindle.

137. Meadows and Wright, *Thinking in Systems*, 76.

138. Meadows and Wright, *Thinking in Systems*, 77.

139. Fiksel, *Resilient by Design*, 4.

140. Walker and Salt, *Resilience Thinking,* chap. 6, Kindle.

141. Bruce M. Braes and David Jonathan Brooks, "Organisational Resilience: Understanding and Identifying the Essential Concepts," in *WIT Transactions on the Built Environment, Safety and Security Engineering IV*, vol. 117 (SAFE 2011, Antwerp, Belgium: WIT Press, 2011), 117–28, https://doi.org/10.2495/SAFE110111.

142. Fiksel, *Resilient by Design*, 84.

143. Meadows and Wright, *Thinking in Systems*, 79-80.

144. Kahneman, *Thinking, Fast and Slow*, 81.

145. Meadows and Wright, *Thinking in Systems*, 88.

146. Meadows and Wright, *Thinking in Systems*, 72.

147. Doug Silsbee, *Presence-Based Leadership* (Asheville, NC: Yes! Global, Inc, 2018), chap. 11, Kindle.

148. Jennifer Garvey Berger and Keith Johnston, *Simple Habits for Complex Times: Powerful Practices for Leaders* (Stanford, California: Stanford Business Books, 2015), 71-73.

149. Berger and Johnston, *Simple Habits for Complex Times,* 71-73.

150. Berger and Johnston, *Simple Habits for Complex Times,* 71-73.

151. Berger and Johnston, *Simple Habits for Complex Times,* 71-73.

152. Theodore Scaltsas, "A Cognitive Trick for Solving Problems Creatively." *Harvard Business Review Digital Articles* (May 4, 2016), 2–5.

153. Art Markman, "Your Team Is Brainstorming All Wrong." *Harvard Business Review Digital Articles* (May 18, 2017), 2–4.

154. David Deutsch, *The Beginning of Infinity: Explanations That Transform the World* (New York: Viking, 2011).

155. Deutsch, *The Beginning of Infinity: Explanations That Transform the World*.

156. T. Wedell-Wedellsborg, "Are You Solving the Right Problems?" *Harvard Business Review* 95, no. 1 (January 2017), 76–83.

157. Kaufman, *Poor Charlie's Almanack*, 66.

158. "Economic Moat," *Morningstar* (accessed May 2, 2020), https://www.morningstar.com/InvGlossary/economic_moat.aspx

159. Michael Sony, "Implementing Sustainable Operational Excellence in Organizations: An Integrative Viewpoint." *Production and Manufacturing Research: An Open Access Journal* 7, no. 1 (2019), 67–87, https://doi.org/10.1080/21693277.2019.1581674.

160. John S. Mitchell, *Operational Excellence: Journey to Creating Sustainable Value.* (New Jersey: Wiley, 2015), 9.

161. Robert D. Miller, Jacob Raymer, Randall Cook, and Shaun Barker. "The Shingo Model for Operational Excellence." *Shingo Institute, Utah State University* (2013), http://sapartners.com/wp-content/uploads/2014/04/ShingoModelHandbook.pdf.

162. Miller, Raymer, Cook and Barker, "The Shingo Model."

163. Miller, Raymer, Cook, and Barker, "The Shingo Model."

164. Kaufman, *Poor Charlie's Almanack,* 65.

165. James O'Loughlin, *The Real Warren Buffett: Managing Capital, Leading People* (London; Yarmouth, ME: Nicholas Brealey Pub., 2004), 168.

166. Rosling, Hans, Ola Rosling, and Anna Rosling Rönnlund. *Factfulness: Ten Reasons We're Wrong about the World--and Why Things Are Better than You Think,* first edition (New York: Flatiron Books, 2018).

167. Helen Hasan, and Alanah Kazlauskas. "The Cynefin Framework: Putting Complexity into Perspective" (2014), 55–57.

168. Schmidt, Eagle and Rosenberg, *How Google Works,* 198.